I WANT TO COMMUNICATE, THROUGH THE SHARING OF MY EXPERIENCE, THAT THE ANSWER IS NOT TO RUN OUT ON THE PROBLEM. WITH DIVORCE SO PREVALENT TODAY, I WANT TO SPEAK OUT FOR COMMITMENT TO MARRIAGE.

Something Worth Saving

MYRNA MARSHALL

LIVING BOOKS
Tyndale House Publishers
Wheaton, Illinois

Second printing, June 1987

Library of Congress Catalog Card Number 86-51398
ISBN 0-8423-6068-9
Copyright 1987 by Myrna Marshall
All rights reserved
Printed in the United States of America

To JIM,
*who refused to let go,
in spite of me.
Thanks. . . .*

CONTENTS

ONE
And So, I Begin Again 11

TWO
The Morning After 25

THREE
It Wasn't Always Like This 41

FOUR
Miss Fixit, the Supreme Mender 57

FIVE
But We Don't Have Any Problems 69

SIX
The Lawyer 79

SEVEN
Packing 87

EIGHT
Moving Back 99

NINE
Making It Work 107

TEN
Women Who Left, Women Who Stayed 117

ELEVEN
I Started to Pray 127

TWELVE
The Encounter 137

THIRTEEN
Crash Course in Communication 143

EPILOGUE
The Way It Is 151

Preface

I felt scared, but free. Nervous, but excited. LONELY. Everything I thought of connected to Jim. I kept thinking of what he'd say or do. I wanted to share my new experience with him. Ironic?

I had always thought I could do anything if I tried hard enough. Although it felt strange—only one night—I hated to give up on my new life. But I wasn't sure it would work. I didn't feel the thrill I thought I would upon being alone, on my own.

In this book I want to share the trauma, even one night's worth, with other married women. I want to communicate, through the sharing of my experience, that the answer is not to run out on the problem. With divorce so prevalent today, I want to speak out for commitment to marriage.

Some of the names and minor details have been changed in order to maintain the privacy of individuals in the telling of my story.

ONE
And So, I Begin Again

I had remembered to pack extension cords, giving them an importance not attached to the books, records, photographs, family glassware, and coffee I'd left behind. Funny what you grab when you're on your way out the door. Funny what you forget. But I didn't feel funny. I had closed the door on twenty-three years of marriage as if I was going to a movie. I had sounded it out with each one of our four grown children, but never mentioned it to Jim. *Would the kids come to see me?* My stomach flip-flopped from the time I'd driven out of the driveway. *Was this what I wanted?* Suddenly, I didn't know.

I sat in the only chair in the bedroom. This was my first apartment. I had run away only twenty miles, but it would be a new life, away from our log cabin in the remote upstate New York countryside. I would call each of our four grown children in the morning, and let them know where I was.

Everyone called this a city, but the 9,800 people who lived here thought of it as a town. I had come here often. Every time I made the thirty-minute drive from home before, I wrote a list of things that needed to be bought, picked up, or accomplished. This was the closest thing to a city I'd lived near. Now it was my home.

My apartment was on the ground floor, and the oversized windows in the living room looked out onto the busy, trafficked street. Off-the-street parking in the back alley made my new home even more attractive, since there was a parking space for each one of the tenants (the tenants being the couple upstairs and me).

I looked at the fruits of my twenty-three years of marriage: a four-poster reproduction I had bought at a garage sale; a pewter-looking lamp I had redeemed with S & H Green Stamps; Aunt Eunice's hand-sewn, blue-and-white quilt; a hope chest Dad had given me for my last birthday. (Dad was really his dad, but after all these years he seemed as if he were mine, too.)

"I can't afford antiques," Dad had said. "But I can buy you old things." He'd headed to garage sales, flea markets, and auctions, and had bought a good share of the things I loved.

The bed displayed my many clothes—endless pairs of shoes, winter coats, hats, accessories, sweaters, slacks, blouses, and skirts. I had brought boxfuls of the scarves, necklaces, earrings, and bracelets that would match and complete each outfit.

"There isn't anywhere to put anything," I complained, looking into the narrow closet. Piled high, the clothes seemed mountainous—but they were all I had left of a twenty-three-year investment.

I picked up a magazine and took it into the living room, looking for a coffee table to put it on. There wasn't one. I settled in the recliner he'd bought me last Christmas. I didn't have much, but it was mine.

I wouldn't have taken anything that belonged to him, certainly not the TV. The main thing he'd miss would be the television. Now he could watch it all the time. He wouldn't have to listen to me anymore. So many times I'd tried to talk about what bothered me: our not communicating, my wanting to go out more, his not going to church with me. I'd always taken the kids and gone to church alone, but Jim wouldn't go. He didn't *believe*, he said. I used to wish he'd go anyway, so I didn't have to go alone.

I pulled down the cracked, white window shades. The spring sprang and the shades settled haphazardly at crooked angles. I studied the three doors entering the living room, and tried to determine how I would arrange more furniture if I had some.

My organ fit into the wall opposite the French

doors as if it belonged there. What a fight we'd had about that organ.

"You can't even play it!" he complained.

"I'll take lessons," I argued.

I'd gotten the settlement check from the insurance company and gone shopping. The money was no substitute for the whiplash I received in a head-on collision three years before, but it was all that was offered, so I accepted it. I meant to put the check in the bank for our dream trip to Hawaii. That's what I told Jim I'd do.

Then I saw the ad: "Automatic rhythm, drums, double keyboard, tape recorder, earphones"—the works. I went to the music store and played their advertised special. I bought it! I didn't think about how mad he'd be until I got home with the organ in the back of the truck. He said he couldn't figure me out.

I enjoyed playing that organ. I couldn't have left it behind, now. He wouldn't want it, anyway. He said every time he looked at it, it reminded him of the way I did whatever I wanted.

Apartments like this were built for tall people, I thought, as I walked into the bathroom and looked up at the medicine cabinet. It was on a wall next to the bathtub. The only shelf in the room was tucked into a corner over the toilet. Not what you'd call an efficiency apartment.

Walking from the bathroom, I marveled at the kitchen's empty enormity. The refrigerator was a full twelve feet from the elbow-high, cast-iron sink. A former tenant had thoughtfully left behind a pink gingham skirt with stretched elastic, hanging lopsided from the sink. There was no stove (a blessing in disguise, because I could put my hot pot on the metal hutch that edged up next to the sink, saving me the eight-foot walk across the wooden floor).

I dragged my one garage-sale kitchen chair to the pantry in the far corner. Standing on the chair, I put away my few dishes on the shelves I could reach.

My cupboards were little better than bare. I could pick up what I needed at the discount store, which was open until 10:00 P.M. With boxes of clothes strewn around the bedroom, my small amount of kitchen equipment put away, the bathroom settled but empty, I left.

I got to the store and hurried in. I wasn't in the mood to dawdle over shopping as so often was my habit. I zipped around the store, picking up things I designated as necessary: toaster oven, bath mat, towels, shower curtain, drink mix, cereal, milk, envelopes of instant soup, and a small jar of instant coffee. Not everything, but a start.

I stood in what must have been the longest, slowest checkout line in the store, and paid for my "groceries."

I would need gas before driving to work in the morning. I pulled into a service station and studied all the signs—Regular, Unleaded, Super, Diesel—oh yes, the Regular. *Which side of the car is the tank on?* I'd never noticed. I drove up to the pump, taking a chance, and guessed incorrectly. I could barely stretch the hose to make it reach.

Reading the instructions on the pump carefully, I clicked on the proper switch. Nothing happened. I took the hose out, dripping the previous customer's leftover gas on my tennis shoes. Looking knowledgeably into the hose and seeing no gasoline (good thing), I inserted it again. I clicked the switch that said On and tried again. Nothing.

Looking overhead, I saw the sign. In the Evening Hours, Please Pay in Advance.

By this time, I was certain the attendant inside was laughing, as he watched me attempt to decipher all the instructions. I was also sure he could tell this was the first time I'd been out on my own.

I went in and paid. He suggested that next time I might drive in from the other direction so the hose wouldn't "be so rigid in the proper orifice." (Certainly.)

I went back outside, ready to do my stuff. The sudden announcement of Pumps on! blared from the overhead speaker, and I jumped. I hoped no one was watching.

Being in my mid-forties and not knowing how to operate a gas pump did not give me a feeling of confidence and intelligence. The task seemed like one of those that all women should be taught at night school, like how to change a flat tire and check the oil. It looks good, too, when you're stranded by the side of the road, to at least know where to find your dipstick.

I had to do things for myself now. "If I have to do it, I can," I said to the dripping hose, watching it spill gas onto my shoes again and into my purse, which was on the ground next to my feet.

I went inside and paid the extra amount for the underestimated tank of gas. I was thankful I owned a compact car. If I had to rely on my own paycheck now, I'd have to save money everywhere I could. "Bite the bullet," Jim would say.

The attendant took my extra coins and stepped back quickly, wrinkling up his nose. I realized that the familiar but unpleasant odor was coming from me. Gasoline is one of the most pungent colognes.

I drove back to the apartment, carried in my bags, then pulled the car around to the alley behind the building. It was spooky. The streetlight had been broken, and suddenly I was aware of how alone I was. Though this town was virtually crime-free, I remembered television news stories about people getting mugged or molested in dark parking lots. My imagination ran away with my peace of mind. For a moment, I wished Jim was here. He would never have left me alone in a place like this. I got out of the car and locked all the doors, marveling that we had never done that in the rural area where we lived. Sometimes we left the keys in the ignition overnight.

It felt like Christmas as I unpacked my purchases, except there was no one there to share the

SOMETHING WORTH SAVING

fun of what I'd bought. These were necessities, though; I needed the toaster oven in lieu of a stove that wasn't there. When I could save enough money, I'd buy a stove in one of those secondhand shops. Until then, I could cook TV dinners and pot pies, and make toast. The hot pot would suffice for canned spaghetti, soup, and coffee.

I stepped back, feeling pretty thrifty. Jim had always told me how good I was at stretching money. He'd be proud of me now. (Maybe not right now.)

I put everything away and hung up the matching shower curtain, bath mat, and towels. The bathtub looked so inviting, I decided to shed my dirty clothes and step in. I loved to stand in a hot shower and warm my arthritic bones and tired muscles, letting the heat steam its way into my spirit. I always looked forward to that at home. We'd installed a new bathroom with temperature-set faucets, controlled for even and consistent heat. When it came to plumbing fixtures, Jim, being a plumber, believed in getting the best.

Not so, these faucets—they dripped. When they finally came on, a blast of cold water coated my aching bones with more aches. I got the water temperature stabilized and reentered the shower. Ah . . . finally . . . soothing heat, pleasant . . . but wait! Another blast of icy water! There was no controlling the temperature. It jumped back and forth between cold and steaming hot until I felt as

And So, I Begin Again

if I were in the throes of a medieval torture test. The test worked—I surrendered and got out. I'd have to wash my hair in the tall kitchen sink in the morning.

If Jim were here, I thought, *he'd give me a back rub*. Starting with my shoulders, then my stiff neck, he'd massage my sore muscles with his strong hands, working all the way down my calves to my feet—the final ecstasy—rubbing each toe, one by one.

But he's not here, stupid—he doesn't even know where you are. How could I figure he'd be here, when I left to get away from him? When I walked out while he was gone, so he wouldn't know where I was going?

I dried off and got ready for bed. I was goose-pimply cold. I'd have to get the landlord to turn on the heat. It was chilly for September. Good thing I'd packed my nightgown in my purse. I found the gown at a rummage sale. It was the first flannel one I'd bought in at least twenty-four years—I'd never needed one before.

But this isn't like before, I reminded myself—*I'm beginning again*.

Coffee would warm me up. I found the coffee, but no cream, so I had to drink it black. I poured the steaming water into my cup and settled down on the bed, drinking the coffee in the most comfortable spot in the apartment.

Sitting there in the dark, I noticed the streetlight outside my window. We owned ten acres at

SOMETHING WORTH SAVING

home, in pitch-black privacy at night. The *hoo-hoo* of the owl sang us to sleep and the chattering sparrows cheered us awake. We never thought of giving up our solitude for city efficiency and busy streets. We agreed on that, anyway. We wondered how city people could stand it, not having any place to move, run, walk, or listen.

I could hear the traffic zooming by on the street outside the living room. It was almost midnight. Didn't these people ever go to bed?

It was strange to be in bed alone. We'd curled up together every night for twenty-three years, except for baby sabbaticals and hunting trips. After the problems put a strain on us, we lay in bed, trying not to touch each other.

The bed was cold. I wasn't used to that. When things were different before we started arguing, he'd go to bed five minutes ahead of me to warm up my side. He'd lie there and move over when I was ready to climb in. In our northern winters, that felt good. We could have bought an electric blanket, but it was nice to start off a night like that—curling up close and warm to each other. I appreciated his bed-warming gesture as much as anything else he did.

I stretched out my short legs and brushed the entire width of the sheet with my toes. I used to think how nice it would be to stretch out and enjoy the whole bed. But it felt too big, and it felt very empty. It didn't feel that great.

What am I doing here? I have a comfortable

And So, I Begin Again

home, my own bed, dishes, everything fixed like I want. Yet here I am, sitting in a bedroom with no shades on the windows, taking a shower in a bathroom with hot-and-cold-running surprise. Will this ever look like home? Will it ever be lived in, comfortable, the way my log cabin was? Were things really that bad? Had I made a mistake?

I had left the cabin in a hurry. I was afraid to look back at the porch where we'd sat and watched the rain and listened to the low *garrumm* of bullfrogs, the lawn where we'd had picnics, the pond where we'd swum. So many good memories. They stood out more now than the bad times. I knew I couldn't leave if I had to think of these things. I'd thought enough already.

One summer night a year ago, during a heavy rainstorm, we secluded ourselves on the porch, wrapped in a blanket, swaying back and forth on the glider. It had been dry. Most of our neighbors' crops were dying, and rain was prayed for everywhere.

It began in late afternoon, about five o'clock. After supper it was still raining, but steady and light. It wouldn't hurt anyone's gardens, wash away any crops. Jim and I thought it would be a nice way to spend the evening, watching the rain.

I took our coffee out on the porch, and we drank it as we watched. Our old inner tube rested on the bank of the pond, which was left almost empty from the hot, arid summer. There was just enough water along the bottom to provide for the thirty trout that Jim had purchased and put there.

The rain picked up, larger drops hitting the roof and the railing on the porch, creating bigger circles in the pond. We sat there, dry under the porch roof, wrapped tightly in the blanket, rocking on the glider, watching it all.

"It'll be another two hours before that tube begins to float," Jim said. We bet each other a dollar on the exact time it would happen, when the tube would become waterborne and slide off the bank into the fresh, clean, rain-watered pond.

"Remember when we sat until the tube floated?" Jim asked a month later, as we sat watching another rainstorm. We had special times, once.

He should be home from bowling by now. I was worried about what he'd do when he found my note. I knew he wouldn't be surprised, though I never had come right out and pinpointed the specifics. He would know, I was sure of that. Even he couldn't miss our problems. He was not known for being sensitive, but he knew about my confusion. I'd been telling him I wanted to talk, to communicate.

My unhappiness showed, my friends told me. He had to be mighty dense to miss it.

I gave up on trying to convey it to him. He'd come back at me with an argument, and I'd turn my back and say it didn't matter. But it did. Inside, it made me boil. Resentment and anger fed each other like an eternal flame. I didn't bother to tell him most of what I felt. I thought that it

And So, I Begin Again

would only end up the same, that it would never matter to him. I had formed answers to questions never asked, never said out loud to him.

I began to live in an oblivious state, waiting for the right time for me to take care of me. I embraced a mental singleness. I knew he didn't care about me, so I'd care about myself. All these things were in my thoughts as I pictured him finding the note. In my mind, that's all it took—a note. Not much to cancel a marriage after twenty-three years.

"I need to feel close," I'd told him. I had a need, but I couldn't make him see it. We didn't have the closeness, it seemed.

We'd always done things together—gone for rides, taken the kids on picnics. But we didn't talk. He never seemed to wonder what was inside me. I'd never gotten close to him in that way. Talking, communicating—that was important to me.

I wanted us to have a relationship that was open, one in which you could say what was on your mind or what was bothering you. Honest comments. Not getting into accusations or blame, but feelings—the internal workings of people—us.

He would listen, then I, as I pictured it; and at least we would know how the other perceived life. I wanted it to work both ways, so that we could describe to each other the way we really felt. I hoped that eventually we would know how each other thought and felt without having to speak a word. But without the communication, I felt extra, unnecessary, as if what I thought didn't matter. I told him all these things and he laughed. "You read too much," he chuckled. "You see that on television?" He said that once, after I wished aloud that we could set aside regular times for conversation. Maybe I said it wrong. Maybe I asked too often. But as I lay alone that night in my apartment, separated from my husband, I knew I had needed that. He hadn't believed me. Maybe now he would.

I finished my coffee and closed my eyes, wondering if I'd ever get used to that streetlight shining through my bedroom window.

He would come in the door downstairs, put his bowling ball in the coat closet, and walk up the stairs to the living room, whistling all the way. I used to like to hear him coming. He sounded so happy. Tonight he'd whistle until he saw my note.

He would read it, throw it on the kitchen counter, and go into the bedroom to check my shoes. When he counted, and calculated I'd taken more than half of my fifty-one pairs of shoes, he'd believe it. He'd swear, throw something across the room, and turn on the TV. He'd get a glass of iced tea and sit down.

That's what I figured, lying there in my first apartment, drifting off to sleep. I guess I didn't know Jim like I thought. . . .

TWO
The Morning After

I got up early and washed my hair in the kitchen sink. The cold water was not limited to the bathroom, I discovered, as ice water dripped down my neck and back. I finished quickly, and briskly towel-dried my hair, mostly for heat and stimulation.

I plugged in my trusty hot pot and fixed a cup of coffee. *Blech!* Leftover instant coffee—something I'd never allowed in my kitchen.

But this was my kitchen, now, wasn't it? I'd bought cereal and milk but forgotten the sugar. I ate my breakfast, such as it was.

I had to hurry or I'd be late for work. I dressed in the only outfit I could spot in a hurry. I felt like I was vacationing alone. It was strange not to have anyone there to zip me up or tell me if my slip showed.

I would have to learn to plan for the extra

SOMETHING WORTH SAVING

fifteen minutes I'd need to get to work on time. Work was further from here than it was from our log cabin, and in a different direction. The three points—the cabin, work, and the apartment, were like points of a triangle. There were no shortcuts to work from here, no cutting across corners to get there quicker. The road to my job was the only road. I would just have to remember to leave earlier than I used to.

I'd worked in that small town for nine years, filing, keypunching, running the computer, purchasing, and handling sales. I liked having the various duties. The town had a regional 300-student high school, a local branch of the city bank, a one-man, two-pump gas station, a Mom 'n' Pop grocery store, and the manufacturing plant where I worked. Husband, wife, and eventually children worked at one of those places, usually the plant. In fact, half as many people worked at the factory as lived in the whole village. I knew most of the two hundred employees by name, and I enjoyed those with whom I worked closely in the office. They would be surprised when they heard I'd left home.

I got the keys off the nail I'd pounded in by the door, and I locked up the apartment.

The car was still in the alley, untouched right where I left it. That was a good sign. I was afraid someone would break the windows and steal something, like you hear happens in the city. I started it up, and off I went.

The Morning After

I'd driven this route many times. Usually it was for a rush appointment to the beauty parlor after work, a shopping trip pushed into my lunch hour, or a job interview like the one I had last winter when I was looking for a higher paying job. I'd always driven over to this small city from work, and either gone home from there or back to work in the village at noon. The drive normally took thirty or forty minutes of careful negotiating around curves, up hills and down. It was a pretty drive, but I'd always been in too much of a hurry to enjoy it. This morning was no different, except I was driving to work from the city for the first time—from my own place.

We had come to this city many times. It was full of turning points for me, and for our family. We came once for an antique car show that showed off the cars of the fifties that Jim and I loved. We came for a tractor pull, the first one I ever saw, and I got so excited I ran down the track alongside the deafening jet-powered machine. I covered my ears and loved it!

We went to movies and to dinner here. I laughed, recalling the time at the Chinese restaurant when I forgot to put in my lower partial plate. I had to munch beaver-style during the six-course dinner.

It occurred to me, driving to work that first morning on my own, that this city wasn't a stopping-off place anymore. It was my final destination at the end of the day. It was my home. And this really was the first day of the rest of my life.

I rounded the curve in the road and thought of our four children, whom I'd brought over these hills to get driver's permits on those magic sixteenth birthdays. I'd taught our daughter Denise how to drive along this road. I remembered telling her, "Imagine there are deer or cows around the next curve or in the middle of the road. Think how you'd stop or where you'd drive to avoid them." One Saturday that fall, as she drove around a curve, she met a herd of deer. Denise steered quickly but safely to the shoulder and stopped on the flat patch of grass next to it.

She turned to me. "How did you know?" Never again was it necessary to impress her with the things a mother knows.

My mind was closing doors as I continued the drive. Things would change, I knew that. I wouldn't know my neighbors in the city. In the country, neighbors are essential. As I answered the telephone one day last October, I heard, "Got any apples?" It was my friend Marion. She never bothered to say hello. Whenever I picked up the phone or opened the door, it signaled my hello, and her conversation began.

"I've got some apples here. I'll bring them over. I made us a pie but I don't have enough lard to make one for you. I don't want them wasted. Will you use them?"

She was neighborly and helpful, but not always tactful. I loved Marion. She was a friend, but was

The Morning After

also like another mother. Age didn't come between us. I would have to call Marion and let her know I'd moved.

I slowed to make the sharp turn into the parking lot at work. Every time I saw the sign, Parking Lot, I laughed, recollecting the day last year when our new boss arrived.

"Parking lot? You call this driveway a parking lot? You'd be lucky to get seven cars in here. And then one of them had better not want to go home early. Some parking lot," he muttered, shaking his head as he walked away.

I pulled into the last available space. I didn't see Jim's van right away. I got out and walked down the sidewalk to the front door.

Jim drove along beside me and stopped. I looked at him, but I wasn't prepared for his face—the face I'd seen so many times, buried in the newspaper, watching TV, peering over a malfunctioning motor. It was pulled apart with pain, lines creasing deeply into his cheeks, anguish welling over from his eyes. I didn't think he'd mind my leaving, as long as I didn't take the TV.

"Where've you been?" he said. "I've been driving around all night. I couldn't find you."

I hadn't thought he'd look for me. He was such a nonvisual, nonverbal person, I never thought my leaving would matter. As I looked at him, I realized I was wrong. He was torn. Tears ran down his face. He made no effort to wipe them away. His whiskered face and red eyes attested to the fact that he hadn't been home to shave, shower, or sleep.

The note had provided an easy way to handle the whole thing. I didn't know what to tell him in person. Everyone else talks about leaving. On soap operas they simply announce it and pack a few things. It all works out somehow. I hadn't thought about this physical part of leaving, the confrontation, facing each other with the most painful news you can share, trying to be civil and reasonable.

Life is not a television script, I learned. It may be that way in the movies, but it doesn't mean it'll be that way in your home, or in your mind. Leaving was agonizing to both of us. I had prepared myself for it, but Jim had not had any warning.

He looked awful. In all the years of kids' troubles, money problems, and sickness, I had never seen him cry.

"What happened?" he asked.

How could I explain in one sentence the frustration, the anger, the resentment? "I wasn't happy," I said.

"With what?"

"With so many things. We got so that even though we lived together, I didn't feel together. I couldn't stand another twenty years of being in a rut, not being close. I had to change it. I had to get out."

"Let's talk."

The Morning After

"Talk?" After all the years of his silence, he wanted to talk? I had wanted to talk so many times. Now he was ready?

"If you did this to get my attention, it worked," he said gently.

I hadn't. I didn't think about playing games. I only knew what I needed to do to make me become a whole person again. Nothing I had experienced or explained seemed to matter to him—and I needed to know I mattered to him.

He opened the door of the van and tried to smile. "You want to talk?" he said. I got in, closing the door. He started the engine and we drove about half a mile up the hill to a parking spot along the road and stopped.

"I didn't think you'd care," I said. I really didn't. But how could I have thought he wouldn't care? Because I hadn't been thinking about him, that's how. I'd been thinking about me, how I felt, not how he would feel.

I was convinced he wouldn't believe I would stay away, that he'd think I had just wanted to teach him a lesson. I waited for him to make the usual accusation—"Is this another one of your dumb acts?" But it didn't come. Usually, when I said something, he listened with half an ear and said, "Uh-huh." I was so used to a response of virtually no magnitude that I wasn't prepared for his deep response now.

"I called the office to talk to you at 8:00, 8:15, 8:20, and 8:30," he said, the tears creating a rivulet through his whisker stubble. "You weren't in," they said. I was afraid they were just telling me that because they knew you didn't want to see me. I thought everyone here must've been in on it. So I got in the car and drove down. When I didn't see your car, I got scared all over again."

Jim looked out the window, pressing his moist cheek against the glass. He clenched his fist and leaned his chin on it, deep in thought. "For the first time," he continued, "I realized you might have left town. I thought I wouldn't have another chance. I was sure you had left forever, that it was over. I waited there awhile. I didn't know where else to go. I knew I'd never see you again." This came out like a shot, from a spot inside him I'd never known. He was still crying, and he made no effort to wipe away the tears that ran down his cheeks and landed on his shirt.

"But it's just eight o'clock now," I said, totally out of context, realizing something was amiss. Where did the time go? "What time is it?"

"It's almost ten now."

My first day on my own and I had overslept.

"You forgot the clock radio." His mouth tried to make a smile, but his face wouldn't cooperate. "I haven't been to bed. I've been driving around trying to find you. I went everywhere I thought you'd ever been, and I couldn't find the car anywhere. I got so worried."

Suddenly changing directions, he asked, "Why?

The Morning After

Why did you go? We didn't have any problems that big."

He'd said it many times. "That's the way people are," he'd say. But I didn't care if every other couple in the world watched television, didn't talk, didn't get to know each other. That wasn't the way I wanted us to be. I told him I wanted conversation. He listened with one ear and watched TV with both eyes, so I quit trying.

I tried to talk during the last five or ten years, when I needed communication, tenderness, and understanding. And now he was asking me what happened? I'd attempted to convey my confusion and frustration, and he was telling me we didn't have problems?

I'd thought it was obvious—the arguments we had, my not wanting to be taken for granted, not wanting him to misunderstand me—like the times I cried as we watched movies or television; the laughter I heard from him, telling me, "It's only a story, you know."

As we sat in the van, I shared my sentiments for forty-five minutes. But it wasn't working. He didn't understand what the problem was. *He* didn't have any problems. He listened, but had nothing to offer, no contributing factors he could think of. "It's your mind. They're *your* thoughts," he said. "You'll have to learn to handle it."

He listened, but he didn't hear. As much as I hated to admit it, I could see he was making an honest effort. Watching his face, I knew he sincerely thought there was no problem!

This man had never planned on anything until it happened. He had never had a dream that would change his life. He told me that the only thing he ever wanted was me. Even though I didn't understand his thinking, it's hard to argue with a philosophy in cement like that.

My head was in the clouds; I'd always been a dreamer. But he couldn't understand that. His head and feet were firmly planted on the ground, and I had a problem comprehending the vast thinking that required (or, rather, did not require). He was literal. I was fanciful. He handled life from one instant to the next. I looked at the entire universe and wondered when I'd have time for all of it.

He saw no exciting, whirlwind, ultimate purpose except to live one day at a time and be happy. To him, that meant working, coming home, eating dinner, watching TV, taking a shower, going to bed, making love, and getting up the next morning to do it all again. To me, though, happiness was internal. I wanted more than the routine, the rituals of daily living. "Life is so daily," said my friend Norma. How true.

He and I did not think alike (which I'd always known), but that isn't required in a relationship. I thought in our case a little "alikeness" would've worked wonders, but he fought that. He was not comfortable expressing his emotions aloud. On

The Morning After

the other hand, I knew of no other way to exist and be happy than to spill my guts to neighbors, write loving notes to friends, hug family, smile at strangers. I loved that part of life—communication. What opposites Jim and I were.

I had pictured him being angry after reading the note and going into his regular routine for the late-night news.

Yet, to my surprise, he told me that what he actually felt was despair—the aloneness of knowing that I had chosen not to rely on him anymore; the frustration of not understanding what went wrong; the hurt of not knowing where that someone, with whom he'd slept for over twenty years, was sleeping; the agony of making telephone calls to relatives and friends, and not getting any answers. Do they know and not want to tell me? Are they against me too? What did I do to her to make them turn against me? Whom can I call to find out? If no one knows, how will I find her?"

"I didn't even turn on the TV last night," he said. "I never thought of watching it."

I was so used to having the television monitor our discussions that I came to think of it as a rival. Whenever I wanted to make a particular point, it was blaring. Once I turned off the set so we could talk. "Turn it on," he said, staring at me. "Turn it on," he repeated. There was no emotion in his voice. I felt like the neighbors' beagle being told to heel. I turned the TV back on.

The no-discussion discussion problem was partly my fault. When the time came for a showdown, I backed down. I let him believe that my thoughts didn't matter, that my feelings were not important. I didn't stand up for myself, and at some point I began to accept the role of secondary citizen. If he wanted me to play the happy housewife, I would; if he didn't want to talk, I acted as if it didn't matter. But it did matter. And inside, I fought it.

No one would ever know the real me, I determined. I was so noble that I might have allowed myself sainthood status if anyone had asked. I was performing the duties without acknowledging them. This was not deliberate, however; underneath I resented it, but I consciously hadn't known why. We continued to talk in the van that day, parked in a lovers' lane.

"I wanted to have a companion, a friend," I said.

"And I wasn't? We did everything together. I never wanted to be anywhere but home."

He still didn't get the picture, and our discussion went round in circles. He thought everything was perfect—he was happy, so why wasn't I?

"Doing things together doesn't ensure communication," I tried to explain. "Being next to each other, watching television or eating, does not mean that you know and understand what's bothering you, pleasing you, or making each other tick."

The Morning After

He hadn't slept, and exhaustion kept him from guarding himself any longer. "I can't let you leave. I need you. You're the only one I've ever loved."

I'd never heard him say those things. They sounded good. For the first time in months—years—we were talking to each other. Responding.

His face had formed new wrinkles overnight. He had warmth in his eyes when he looked at me. This must be two other people, I thought. We kissed, and the softness of his lips warmed me. No longer did I feel resentment or bitterness, but the tenderness reminiscent of our ninth-grade dates. He was my special Jim again.

"Would you come home?" he asked. He said it so easily. After the months of wondering and worrying about what I'd be doing with the rest of my life, four words seemed to erase it all, just like that, as if it hadn't happened. He wanted me to forget the whole thing.

I looked at his face again. How could I not listen to him? This was the first time in years he'd asked me to do anything. I was tempted . . . but would it be any different?

"We'll talk more," he said. "I'll listen and try to be more aware of your feelings. But you've got to tell me what they are. You can't pretend they don't matter if they do. You've got to make me know what you feel. Call me any name you want if you need to. Make me listen." Then, quietly, he said it again: "Let's go home."

He wanted me back. It had been only one night, yet our whole life together had been packed into that night. We talked about every little problem I thought was so big. We ironed out my doubts.

I went to the office and apologized to my supervisor for being late. Then I asked to be excused for the day. "Personal," was all I had to say. She knew Jim and I were having problems. Everyone knew. The office must have been buzzing. When you work with seventeen women, the buzzing is inevitable.

I made my decision. I would go back and try again to make it work. I told Jim to meet me back at our house, and we said good-bye. I drove to the apartment and picked up some clothes. Then I drove home.

As I turned into my own driveway, it seemed like years since I'd left, not just a day. I was welcomed into my house with a hug and a kiss. Another hug, then another.

One night alone in my own apartment and I went home. But he had asked me—he wanted me back. That was what mattered.

I had left the furniture at the apartment, though. I had an uneasiness about things that wouldn't let me move everything. The apartment was my security; I hated to let go of that. I didn't want to be pulled into an arrangement that would put me on the spot again. I didn't ever want to

The Morning After

feel that I had no place else to go. I paid for a month's rent.

My few pieces of furniture settled into an empty, echoing apartment and waited for me to make up my mind.

THREE
It Wasn't Always Like This

After I was home, it seemed that I had gotten everyone stirred up over nothing.

But it wasn't "nothing" to me. I had meant it. I would have stayed away, except I saw Jim's face. I couldn't hurt him anymore. I'm supposed to make him happy, not hurt him, I said to myself, remembering the way we used to be. Things weren't always like this.

Jim graduated from high school two years before I did. By the time he joined the navy, we had dated for one prom, four square dances, and a few movies. He came over to my house a few Saturday afternoons, and we would sit on the porch while I talked. He didn't say much. Usually, we just sat there.

We never went steady, so I was surprised when I got Jim's first letter from boot camp. He wouldn't have put anything on paper if he had any choice, but boot camp was far away and long-distance calls cost too much. He wrote some flowery, sweet things that I'd never heard him say out loud. I was his best girl, and he couldn't wait to get home and see me.

I was excited to be getting mail from a sailor. No one else in the junior class ever dated anyone in the service. Jim sent a picture of himself in his dress blues and I showed it off to all my friends. He and I got pretty chummy through the mail, and when he came home on leave, we dated steadily, this time more seriously.

Jim had been a quiet person in high school. Before he joined the navy, he smiled, but didn't say much. He assumed everything in the world was fine unless he heard otherwise, and he took small, daily events for granted. He was content—unobtrusive, you might have called him.

After he joined the navy, he "became a man," as the slogan says. He was more confident and he kidded around more, joking with everyone. We dated more and more. When Jim had leave, he would hitchhike home the three hundred miles from Bainbridge, Maryland, to New York State.

When we decided to marry, he was stationed at Moffett Field, California. The navy gave him eight days' leave for our wedding, and Mom and Dad set us up in a lakeside honeymoon cabin thirty miles away.

On our way to the lake, we drove through a small town, tin cans clanging on the pavement.

It Wasn't Always Like This

We stopped at the only red light. Crepe paper hung from the antenna, and our windows were soaped with messages of "Just Married."

"Sucker!" cried some young boys from the street corner.

"A happy sucker," Jim said, patting my knee. Could anyone else feel as good as we did that night? I didn't think so.

We began our marriage together while separated from the rest of the world. Everyone should be so lucky. Instead of going to Hawaii, Switzerland, or the Bahamas, couples should hole up in a lonely cabin on a quiet lake, with nothing to distract them but a troop of Boy Scouts next door and a couple of amorous cats howling their love calls from the dock.

I learned to "cook" in those few days, relying heavily on tuna-fish sandwiches and chicken noodle soup. Jim didn't complain when I reversed his order and gave him a breakfast of hard eggs and soft bacon. We were in love.

We hardly went outdoors except at night, to walk down to the lake and take in the beauty of the water sparkling diamond-like in the moonlight, slapping up against the docked wooden rowboats. The time went by too fast.

"I heard it'll be Hawaii," Jim said. "You'll be able to go with me." He packed his duffel bag as I sat on the bed and watched. He was getting ready to report back to the West Coast for his next assignment. "Hawaii?" I bounced up and down on

SOMETHING WORTH SAVING

the bed. "I've never been there! I'll love it!" We chattered away about our living quarters, the weather, the extended honeymoon we'd have living there. We left the lakeside honeymoon cabin and stayed with his folks in the upstairs bedroom he'd used alone only a week before. Two days later, he left for California.

I moved in with his family while we awaited the military paperwork and red tape. With his parents, I could avoid loneliness and quell Jim's fears for me while he was gone. I was with them when I got the news from Jim: Hawaii was scrapped. True to naval surprise, Jim would spend the next ten months on board the aircraft carrier U.S.S. *Saratoga* in its home port of Jacksonville, Florida. When I heard that, I wanted to move near the base and get an apartment. I wanted us to be together, even if only during weekend passes.

"You'll be alone when we're out at sea," Jim worried. "You'd better stay where you are." So I continued to live with his folks.

His family was at once mine. His mom, Theo, was fun to be with, talk to, get to know. She became one of my best friends. She was available to talk, most of the time, and she didn't insist on my doing things her way. She believed in helping young people get started but letting them do things on their own.

Before Jim had gone on board ship, Theo had let us use the bed upstairs. It was hollowed out in

It Wasn't Always Like This

the middle from years of use, making it impossible for us to go to bed angry. We would lie on the side of the bed and roll right into each other. We ended up laughing, then making love. When Jim left, I moved downstairs to a single bed.

I wasn't to be alone for long. I discovered I was pregnant and was thankful to be living with Theo, a four-time authority on the physical changes I experienced. Months later, Jim's ship was in port in Florida when Diana was born. He managed to get two extra days added to his weekend pass, and he hitchhiked the twenty hours home to see his new daughter. I was still in the hospital when he arrived, and we had quite a reunion—we were a family now. He was in the room when the nurse brought in the baby for her feeding. He got to hold her in his dress blues, even though the nurse beheld him as if he were transmitting a deadly virus. His time was too short, but at least he got there. He was gone all too soon, and then it was home with my in-laws to learn how to take care of a new baby.

Excitement prevailed throughout the house, yea, the nation. Diana was the first grandchild. She was also the first girl in the family in what must have been a thousand years. It seemed that way from the attention she received. Any time of day we were likely to have visitors who wanted to see how she'd grown, if she had a tooth, if she had curly hair (or if she had any hair).

I never had any privacy after that, and I had

trouble nursing the baby. I hadn't been brought up to have my bedroom like Grand Central Station while I had half my clothes off.

"Diana is all I have," I explained to my new mother. "I like to take care of her myself. With so many people coming in and picking her up, fussing with her, I don't have time to be with her." I felt possessive and jealous over the time I had with my small baby, and Theo understood.

Soon I started looking for somewhere else to live. It wouldn't be easy, though, because I had no job or income except for Jim's seventy-five-dollar monthly allotment check. His mom and dad as well as my own were aware of my frustration. They didn't agree with my philosophy, but they knew how important it was to me and tried to understand. Though I wasn't aware of it, they decided to help.

One Sunday I took the baby to church, and Jim's folks said they would meet me for a picnic afterward. I noticed that the directions they gave me led to the motel that my own mom and dad owned and had rented to travelers since I'd been in my teens. *Maybe we're all going on a picnic together*, I thought, driving there from the church. As I pulled into the drive I noticed that my in-laws had already arrived and stood on the small front porch next to my own mom and dad. I had made many a bed at this place, and mitered many a corner, tucking it in just so, pleasing both my mother and the tourists.

It Wasn't Always Like This

We walked inside the end cabins, which had been numbers one, two, and three. What a change! They had knocked out the walls between the three units and combined them into one small but very cute apartment. Number one became the kitchen and dining area. Number two, the living room and bathroom. Number three was the bedroom and closet.

"You've done wonders with this," I marveled. "You've converted them into apartments?" Yes, they said. Two more apartments had been made out of numbers four, five, and six, and seven and eight. A state expressway replaced what had been the country highway that ran in front of the hotel. As a result, tourist traffic died down, so Mom and Dad went with the times. (My folks were usually with 'em or ahead of 'em.)

"Good idea." I went from room to room, giving assessment and approval. When I turned around, they all were looking at me.

"It's for you," Theo said. Her face broke into a wide grin, and she gave me a breath-squeezing bear hug. "We know you want your own place. It's close enough to see your folks, and only fifteen minutes from us. We can come and see the baby—but we'll call first. We all got together and fixed it up because we want you to be happy."

I noticed the round oak table that had been stored in the attic next to our bedroom. The chairs I had seen hanging up on nails in the barn. I recognized the blonde bookcase bed as one I had made up just a few years before.

They had pooled ideas, efforts, furniture, and money to give me something I wanted. The rent, a whopping thirty-five dollars a month, I learned later, had been paid for two months. I felt special and loved—these were very nice people, my four parents.

Diana and I moved in with our few supplies, and it was fun playing house in my own house. Meanwhile Jim's ship was called overseas for standby during the 1957 Lebanon crisis. He had been at sea for eight months and standing by in Lebanon for another month. His shipboard duty was coming to a close, and the months of waiting and separation were almost over. Jim soon would be discharged from the navy, and I couldn't wait.

I began to prepare the apartment for my permanent male visitor. I bought an overstuffed chair at an auction for three dollars. It was a chair into which he could sink and take a nap after work. I got an end table for fifty cents at the same auction and pictured Jim reading in his chair and using the table for his ashtray and newspaper. It was fun to plan on his "moving in." We hadn't been alone together since the honeymoon.

His plane was due at 8:00 A.M. Theo kept the baby overnight so I could get an early start on the hour's drive to the airport. I had made a special dress, two sizes smaller than when he left, and dieted to fit into it. I wanted to look perfect for our big reunion.

It Wasn't Always Like This

I was up bright and early that day. I picked up my cup of coffee and carried it to the bathroom to drink while I put on my makeup. I walked back to the kitchen, and when I came back I couldn't find my coffee, so I fixed myself another cup.

As I drove to the airport, my mind darted like a hummingbird. Here . . . there . . . then *zoom!* Away! I didn't get very good directions. This was the first time I had come here alone; when we came ten months ago, Jim drove.

I could see the airport, the landing strip, the planes, all the activity—but how to get there? I drove on, looking for the road. No road. Having gone too far, I found myself helplessly driving away from the airport. I began to sweat. How could I get over there? Only a fence separated my car from the runway. For a brief moment, I thought of ramming it down and driving down the runway to meet my husband's plane.

I went back and forth in this state of mind until I saw a small sign: Airport—This Way for Detour. I took the turn and at last I was headed that way. Suddenly I realized—his plane had been due twelve minutes ago! I wouldn't know where to look for him. Where would he be now?

I was almost to the parking lot when I saw a sailor, walking. A sailor? No—it was Jim! I stopped the car in mid-traffic, jumped out, ran up to him, and hugged him! Kissed him! It was so good to feel his arms around me. He smelled good—the after-shave aroma I remembered. He even *felt* good. He was home!

On the way back I drove, because Jim said he just wanted to look at me. I was nervous, like it was a first date. We decided to go home first, to be alone. Later we would go to his mom and dad's, to say hello and to get the baby.

Suddenly a siren wailed behind me, signaling a pull-over. When the officer got out and looked us over, though, he relented with a simple request: "Slow down, ma'am—OK?"

I wanted Jim to be there when Diana took her first step, so I'd practically tied her down when she first wanted to walk. I had coaxed her to crawl—sit—anything to stall her from walking for a month.

That day, as we walked in through his parents' front door, Diana studied her daddy curiously. She didn't know who this "Da-Da" man was, but she smiled and tippy-toddled right up to him. He picked up the little girl he hadn't seen for so long, hugged her, and kissed her nose, ears, and tummy. We were a family again.

We lived in our little apartment, with a crib in the corner of our bedroom, until the next year. Eventually, Diana became the older sister of Denise, Joe, and Sarah. Each time the stork flew over, we moved to a bigger apartment. Eventually, we bought a big, old house in a small town eight miles away from where I grew up. The town had changed a little over the years, but closing my

It Wasn't Always Like This

eyes, I could still see The Ladies' Row in the small country church I used to attend. All the women who came to church alone sat on the last row. They looked as if they were lined up for a Sunday social. I expected to see a sign, This Is the Ladies' Row—No Couples Allowed.

Not me, I remember thinking, *I'm not going to end up on the ladies' pew. I'll get married, and my husband and I will sit up front where everyone can see us.*

After settling in that quaint rural village, we walked to services at the United Church, the very one I went to when I was a young girl. Jim never went, though. He always had something to do, or needed that extra hour of sleep. I got used to going alone. With four children I walked to church, pushing two in the rusty Victorian carriage with two walking beside me, each with a little hand holding my skirt tightly on either side. After parking the carriage outside, I strutted my troops right up the aisle of the church, to the second pew. I hoped that someday Jim would go with me. Until then, I would go with the kids.

I recalled reading the church bulletin with all the activities for couples: skiing, bowling, roller-skating, and covered-dish suppers. Five or six couples went every week, husbands and wives, two by two (like on the ark). How I envied them. I wanted to share their fun and fellowship. Maybe another time, I thought.

Even though Jim and I didn't go to church

51

together, we had fun as a young married couple. I wanted to be a wife, the best ever. I played the role eagerly, and enjoyed it. Looking to my man, borrowing his strength for my support . . . I enjoyed being protected, taken care of.

Once a year Theo kept the kids so Jim and I could have a long weekend alone together. We would go to a motel in the next state and enjoy each other. We had always felt special with one another, but on those weekends, we savored feeling young, sexy, and desirable.

Jim worked hard and brought his paycheck home every Friday. He loved to be at home, and never stopped off with the guys or did anything that would keep him away. For us, fifty dollars a week was not rolling in money, but we had enough for what we needed. We made sure we didn't need much.

I stretched a forty-nine-cent package of dried beef in cream gravy into two meals. Hamburger was a four-or-five-nights-a-week staple. I gave Jim three dollars a week from his paycheck and paid bills with the rest. If there was anything left over, we bought ice cream, soft drinks, or M&Ms. That was living.

Once a month I'd surprise Jim and the kids with a special night.

"TV dinners? Wow! Thanks, Mom!"

I let them eat in front of the television on those nights, and later scooted them off to bed so Jim and I could have our own time together. I would make a salad, take a shower, and put on something filmy. Then I'd broil a steak and we'd eat in the living room, TV off, candles lit. The look on Jim's face made it all worth it.

We even enjoyed doing major household chores together such as the garbage. Loading the trash into the back of our old jeep-truck, we all piled in and drove to the town dump. Once there, the kids threw old newspapers over the edge of the hill, one page at a time. I browsed through others' obvious treasures carelessly discarded. Jim took his .22 rifle to the far side of the dump to look for rats. He did his share to diminish the varmint population of the county. If anyone had told me that going to the dump was not an enjoyable afternoon, I'd have given them quite an argument.

We had such fun doing everything together that I assumed Jim and I thought alike. But I was wrong. Jim couldn't understand parts of me—my emotional, sensitive side, the way I looked at life. He didn't know why I thought so much, he said. "Your family has a party for the opening of a flower," he said, kidding about my sentimentality. "It's a national holiday to you when a cat has kittens, not to mention if one dies." I loved celebrating; he was right about that. To me, it was a visible sign of caring. And as a mother, I had four little people I could teach to care, too.

The kids and I loved Christmas. Every year I made a cloth Advent tree, and beginning December 1, each child took turns pinning on an ornament that we'd cut out of greeting cards saved from the Christmas before. We'd make a sugar house out of sugar cubes and confectioner's sugar-and-water "glue" for mortar. Colored frosting and a Necco-wafer roof made a festive, tiny-town addition, and after Christmas I let the kids eat the roof, dust and all.

We strung popcorn and cranberries, munching as we went. No one was permitted to rush Christmas. We oohed and aahed over each present, one at a time. I made a special breakfast from the venison Jim had shot the month before. Jim thought I did too much, bought too much, spent too much. To him, Christmas was a rip-off. But to me, it was a part of a loving, beautiful season. Christmas meant family.

As Jim changed jobs and earned more money, our family outings increased in length and magnitude. The town dump was no longer the only place we could go together as a family. We took the kids camping in the backwoods of Canada. Digging our own latrines, carrying water, and managing each morsel of food needed for two weeks, it was an enjoyable respite from the scheduled routine at home. I learned to cook eggs over the campfire, boil coffee, and take sand out of hot dogs. The kids were little but were required to help. They carried water for dishes and "scouted" for bears. It was fun being together.

Jim and I went deer hunting together once in

awhile, though at first he wasn't fond of the idea. "It's too far for you to walk," he said, his protective head rearing.

"I'm not so stupid that I can't walk," I retorted. But I had to admit it was a lot easier to sit in the clearing and wait for the buck or doe to emerge. Still—

"I drove them right to you," he said. "Why didn't you shoot?"

"They always come from a different direction than I expect. I'm never ready." Apparently, when you're sitting "watch" you're supposed to be prepared at all times, but the cold numbed my toes and fingers. The deer would come charging through the clearing while my fingers were curled up inside my gloves, trying to get some feeling back. Try pulling the trigger when that happens. We had many fights in the woods. And this was supposed to be fun?

Years later Mom said, "You did so many things together. How could you have problems with a man who did that for you?"

No, I thought, remembering her words as I put my clothes back into the dresser out of which I'd taken them only yesterday. *It wasn't always like this. We didn't always have problems. What made us change?*

FOUR
Miss Fixit, the Supreme Mender

I had wanted us to get along, to be one of those couples that inspires music, poetry, and comments from passersby: "How well-suited you are for each other. How great you look together."

I thought any argument was proof that we could not handle it, the worst of all possible faults in a marriage. Not getting along led to even more problems; it was better to back down or quiet down than to reveal my anger. *When people argue,* I thought, *they say regrettable things.* I would never do that, because I wouldn't be able to take the words back. If I got upset, I wouldn't show it. I could handle it. I could get along.

I would go along too, when necessary. I was good at that. Good ole me; I could "appease and please, for those and these" (my self-enforced silent motto). Martyrdom, here I come.

I didn't know the terminology for what I was

doing. I thought it was unselfish, even wonderful of me. Deep down I knew I couldn't argue or fight or call names. It made me physically sick, and by the time my stomach unlocked I couldn't make sense anyway. I would rather run away from a good fight than to listen to one or be in one. I hated watching other people disagree. It threw me into reverse—made me want to leave, run away, get out, just so I didn't have to deal with dissension, name-calling, yelling, confrontation.

When I was upset with Jim, I closed my mouth and said nothing. I got a sick feeling in the bottom of my stomach, but nevertheless I clammed up. I hated to fight. Mom and Dad never did, why should we? I wanted to agree on everything. My husband and I should always agree in order to be happy; I was sure of that. I wanted to do the perfect job of "husbanding." Everyone would know he was mine, blissful and happy, smiling at all times. He would be world-renowned with content, and all because I made it happen! I could do it. I needed to stay on top and be in control, ready and able, on call for fixing up people and situations. If I lost this talent, I didn't know what other ones I might discover I didn't have.

"You think too much," Jim would say, so I tried to stop. "You worry too much." I tried to quit. "Don't do this . . . don't be like that. . . ." I tried not to. I wanted to be the way he liked; the way I was must have been wrong. He kidded me about my tears during sad movies, so I turned my face

Miss Fixit, the Supreme Mender

away from him and tried not to cry. He knew that people in the world were out to get you, so I covered up things I did for friends. I enjoyed teaching Sunday school, but Jim said the church was taking advantage of me. "They'll take your time seven nights a week if you let them," he said. I didn't tell him when I contributed to a door-to-door salesman's college efforts. He would have accused me of being a softy.

I could make him happy if I kept all these things from him. Telling him just caused problems, so I didn't. He didn't need to know my feelings . . . yet I wanted him to want to know, and hoped he would be interested. I hoped he would support me when I volunteered to teach at Vacation Bible School.

"All they want is your time for free. Those kids don't care. They're just in church for the Kool-Aid and cookies. I don't know why you bother."

I began to argue with myself: *I must be wrong, because he's happy and I'm not. I should change.* I would try—I *would* be different. And I continued giving away parts of me that were me, traits I cared about, because I thought that was what he wanted.

Not worrying, I thought, was not caring. Not thinking, a mindless activity. Not this and not that—they were negative responses to a positive attitude I'd had all my life. I began to resent Jim, but how could I tell him? I had done everything with him. He had been my best friend, so I couldn't say those things to him. I might start a fight. I was doing what he wanted, and gradually I began to change into someone else. I wasn't me anymore. I couldn't remember what I was like. I had taken pieces, shreds of myself, and chipped them away.

It usually happened in bed. We would start to argue, and strange things would happen to me. My arms got bigger and bigger. My head started to shrink. It got so small I could watch it disappear. I was outside of my body, observing, vanishing. Soon I was afraid I'd be gone entirely!

I told Jim, and he thought I was nuts. I was scared, and I began to wonder: smaller and smaller, until my head was the size of a tomato ... arms bigger than my head. Was I crazy?

I had set up Jim as head of the family and put myself in a submissive spot. In a way, I created my own monster: he told me what to do because I had asked him to. He was the boss because I established him as such.

I didn't want to be an authoritative, domineering wife. Trying to avoid that, I molded myself into a flexible, easygoing, no-opinion, no-brain, accommodating person. I didn't do it intentionally, but I did it nevertheless.

I was Miss Fixit, an irreplaceable, indispensable, necessary member of anyone's family. I baked bread, made doughnuts, starched and ironed dish towels, and sewed drapes out of old, dyed sheets. I even ironed Jim's shorts. I made all the kids'

Miss Fixit, the Supreme Mender

clothes, slipcovered the furniture, wallpapered, painted, took the kids shopping and on picnics—all with an ever-present smile on my face. I could do it all.

But I *couldn't* do it all.

I began to see that I didn't like the person I was becoming. It was *his* fault. I didn't like to think that, though. I had gone along with him, so guilt told me it was more my fault than anyone else's. I didn't like to think that, either. I lived with that constant conflict, all the while gradually losing my identity, accommodation being my most important product.

In the sixties, when it became popular to "do your own thing" (I listened to all the mottos), the slogans also told women to do what *we* wanted.

"I have to do it; it's my thing," I heard on TV talk shows. Words like *individuality, selectiveness, internal stress, discovery, myself, me,* filled conversations. Discussion centered around *us*—who we are, what we want.

Awareness became the only important thing. This awareness went from us, to me, to I, the *woman!* As years went by, it became less important to do dishes, or to clean and take care of your kids if it interfered with the solitary attitude of wanting to do something for yourself, by yourself. It was almost un-American to deny that self. Burning your bra was just the beginning of thinking of yourself as an important person.

During this era, my thoughts began to blossom.

I did an excellent job at home, and I didn't listen to all the liberated propaganda. But I started wondering about my "own thing."

"Flying an airplane is my thing," said a Hollywood starlet.

"Going back to college and getting my degree is my thing," my sister said, and she proceeded to do so.

What was my thing? I searched my talents, thought of everything that fulfilled me—what I really enjoyed—and came up with what I was already doing. Doing for others? That doesn't count. That's nonsense. Doing for my kids, my husband—sure it's important, but what do I want?

"Find yourself," "Get you own space"—more slogans. This self-examination went on for a decade. My mind delved into life as I continued doing what I knew: taking care of our four grade-school-age children and baby-sitting three more. I had a nursery school at home with fingerpaints, crafts, and lessons. I was superintendent of Sunday school, sang in the choir, baked for the school, sewed for a local television station, took mending and alterations from people in town, and enjoyed every bit of it. Still, I didn't have my own thing.

After much internal mind-searching and discovery, I finally began to know who I was. *Myself*. I settled into a pattern of familiarity with me—what spurred me on, brought me down, excited

Miss Fixit, the Supreme Mender

me, depressed me. How to start my morning, end my day. What an exciting thing to discover, myself. How great to understand me. I didn't like everything I discovered, but I was thrilled to find me.

I didn't fully comprehend that I was Miss Fixit, however, until I was a married, adult mother of four and we got ready to take a ride one Sunday. We packed a picnic for the all-American family outing. I decided that by skipping church I would eliminate any argument about getting a late start. Anytime I wanted to avoid a fight, I could skip church. But I hated to retreat from that one thing; I liked being there.

"You're not going?" Jim said.

"I'll go next week." I was eager to fix any hurt or anger before it arose. (A Supreme Miss Fixit fixes a problem before it occurs. She is anticipatory, thinks ahead, and covers herself before confrontation comes.) I would do just about anything to let things ride, to see people smile. I had a talent for making people happy, I'd been told.

My feeling of being needed came from helping others. I had been helping them for my sake. Not until I sat alone, in my dance-hall-sized kitchen in my first-ever apartment, did I realize how alone I would feel. No one was going to come to me for advice when I couldn't handle my own life.

Being a Miss Fixit has obvious disadvantages. Because I put myself in a position of being depended on, I became a very busy person when no one could do anything without my help. It got so I didn't have time for me. Church, Home Bureau, extra college classes, choir, bowling, all had to be shelved until I was not so busy. When I set myself up as the only one who could fix things, I was allowed to be the one who did.

A necessary position? I've discovered since that it was only a crutch. People close to me needed to know how to fly for themselves, and I should have wanted them to learn to be on their own. Children, friends, parents, husbands, and wives each were meant to do their own thinking. I couldn't do it all for them.

But I set myself up as the expert, and as a result, Miss Fixit had a tremendous responsibility. Isn't this what everyone knew was my best talent? If I couldn't listen and cure a problem, what good was I? Why would anyone want me for a friend? Why would anyone come to me anymore, or talk to me at all? I derived a pleasure from having people bring their pain and their problems to me, because I could help them with the inevitable solution. But if I couldn't fix it, I was a failure. If their problems worked out without me and didn't work out with me, I was useless.

In believing I could do it all, I missed God's point in life. I was trying to help him, to do it *for* him. I was a Christian, and to me that meant going to church, dressing up for Easter, learning the songs for choir and performing them on Sunday.

Miss Fixit, the Supreme Mender

I fixed all my children's problems. I could hear the praise now: "She's so patient and understanding; her kids must think she's terrific. She plays with them, sews all their clothes, cooks wonderful, healthy meals. What a woman!"

My fear of confrontation kept me in charge of everything. I wanted everything to be peachy-keen, hunky-dory and the rest of the sugary, sickening, unreal things that the world isn't. Arguing was not necessary if I did my job properly. Behavior problems with the kids would not happen if I did my job correctly. If our children did something wrong, it had to be my fault.

"She's too young to be dating," Jim said when fourteen-year-old Diana asked permission to go to her first dance.

"She just wants to go out and have fun," I said, trying to run interference for our first-born, first-grown youngster. But by trying to "fix it" for her, all I did was separate her from her dad.

"Try to understand your father," I told her, covering up so he wouldn't get mad. And on and on. . . .

At fifteen she had a grocery bag in hand, stuffed with clothes, and was ready to walk out the door. Jim refused to talk to her. Finally, I told both that they were responsible for their own actions. I could not be the buffer anymore.

That sounded good, said out loud. But inside, I thought I should have done more. She walked down the driveway, her bag still in her arms, and I

SOMETHING WORTH SAVING

agonized. I could have fixed it if I'd hit on the right combination. It had to be my fault.

I kept her from facing the real world. I kept him from facing the real problem with our daughter. We both loved her; we all loved each other. But when you're a Miss Fixit, a Supreme Mender, it's all up to you.

After the kids were in high school, I got a job, thinking, *Maybe this is my thing.* And indeed, I enjoyed working. I was told how great I was just for doing my job. Got paid for doing it, too. But each day it was over when I went home.

And once there, I went back to doing things for people who didn't seem to notice. Yes, a job was my thing!

In nine years with the company, I went from filing, to operating the computer, to purchasing, to telephone sales. I set up a system of sales that officially had not been tried before, and it surprised the boss (and me) at how successful it was. With continued raises, I found my work much more rewarding and fun than sorting laundry or vacuuming.

Meanwhile, as I became more and more aware of my importance at work, I lost sight of the good times I used to have at home. I got so caught up in the fun of office procedure and business logic that I hated to have it end when I went home. I had my own thing!

Daily my mood shifted as I went through the stages: busy, efficient, praised, appreciated at work,

Miss Fixit, the Supreme Mender

to home, making dinner, sitting in front of the TV. Things were in a new, clearer light. Home wasn't that much fun anymore. Things had changed.

I started thinking of me—just me. I took the kids to church each Sunday, and we sang and prayed. When we came home, though, I never discussed the sermon with Jim. He didn't have much use for anything said in church.

I began to wonder what I was doing wasting my life with a man who never appreciated me, who never cared what we did as long as I was nearby when he watched his favorite program. Sewing in the evening was out because the machine made too much noise in the next room. If he was in front of the TV, he wanted me to be there too. In my singular frame of mind, I didn't appreciate it. But being the soother, the accommodator, the adjuster that I was, I never mentioned minding any of it. Inside, I boiled. *Who does he think he is? Don't I have anything better to do than to sit here?*

We went on that way for years. I silently began to accuse him of many things: He didn't love me. He didn't care. And the absolute worst sin—he didn't appreciate me. He wouldn't want to talk about it, so why try?

If I had had to write a theme of "What Went Wrong with My Marriage," I'm not sure I could have. It was gradual, like using too much salt—a habit that starts by using a little one day, then a

67

little too much the next day, then more the next, until the salt becomes the main thing and the food secondary. We became secondary. The going to work, the sitting in his chair became the main thing. Living day to day was a matter of survival. Feed yourself, the kids, him, and off to work. I enjoyed being away more than being home.

I got so used to the way we were that I didn't ask for anything to be different. Some things upset me, but I didn't mention them. This was part of my Miss Fixit attitude surfacing. If I couldn't fix it, who could? So I made sure I could.

But the more I tried, the worse it got. And the worse it got, the more I tried. What a horrible merry-go-round.

It was time to face it. I needed to get off.

FIVE
But We Don't Have Any Problems

Jim had said that to me often enough.

Yet I wondered, *If we don't have any problems, why am I so mixed up? What makes me think I'm unhappy? What's the matter with me? Other women would love to have a husband who wants to stay home.*

Jim worked hard, was proud of his family, and enjoyed his home. My friends had husbands who didn't even want to come home, much less stay there. Patsy told me she'd take Jim anytime. All Arnie ever did was go out. "If I thought I could get him to sit home at night and watch TV, I'd be ecstatic," she claimed.

Dick wandered off to bars on the way home from work, to sit and listen to music. His wife, Doris, would be caught dead before going into any of those places with him. I figured that's why he went, to be away from her. When she finally had enough, she stormed in after him, saying he'd better get home or sleep somewhere else. Last I knew, he was sleeping somewhere else.

What is there about people that makes them want something other than what they have? Maybe it's the adolescence of adulthood.

What brought me to the point of moving out? Looking back on my own experiences, I see certain danger points in any marriage. First, I became unhappy with what I had. Then I refused to let my husband know how I felt. He didn't think we had problems, so I didn't go against him—good ole Miss Fixit. Even though I felt the churning whirlpool drawing me in, I daydreamed into believing all things would be better if I changed my location. Instead of trying to rectify the situation, I thought I could move myself out of our surroundings and—presto!—I would improve. Clinically, logically, coldheartedly, I reasoned all these things on my own. Moving out was the solution. I shed no tears, but not because I wasn't sad; it was necessary for me to be strong and understanding.

I grew cynical. It was hard to respond to my husband in a loving, giving, open way, and I held back. He figured I didn't care. It became a vicious circle of emotions as we accused each other, mentally, of no love at all. Lovemaking without love becomes sex, and sex is not pleasing without love. The day-to-dayness of marriage is not possible without love.

Another danger point is letting others convince

But We Don't Have Any Problems

you of their solution to your problem. Many unhappy marriages are dissolved and new marriages agreed to, but the original problems remain. They won't go away if they've been shoved aside.

Looking to someone else for a solution to one's problems is so normal that it's a way of life. Take, for example, soap operas or movies, books or newspapers. The other side of the fence is always greener, stronger, prettier, thinner, richer, and happier. That someone else looks interesting because he's not the one you have to pay bills with, be sick next to, or ask to zip you into your too-tight dress. I have often wondered how many people would have affairs if the prerequisites were listening to each other chew, burp, hiccup, or scream.

It is normal to think other people are beautiful, that they have no blemishes or problems. The reality is in knowing that's not true. It is normal to think that the afternoon bubble bath floats you off into never-never land, soft and wonderful. The reality is in knowing you have to scrub the tub afterward. Looking at life realistically is the difference between problems and solutions. The ability to find this difference is what saves marriages. But I'm way ahead of myself: We didn't have any problems, he said.

Lunchtime at work was one hour, but we had exceptions, of course. Secretary's Day, someone just hired, someone quitting, someone having a baby—these were all legitimate excuses for celebration and extension of the lunch hour. I hated to miss any of them. If they had a party during lunch hour, I stayed. If the party lasted past 5:00 P.M., I participated. I was a good sport, a friend to all.

One evening I got home at seven, thinking Jim might not notice if I was a little late. He was running the bulldozer, filling dirt into a waterline ditch he'd dug up the day before.

"Sorry I'm late," I apologized, knowing I'd have to listen to him now.

"See that ditch?"

"You have to fill it up?" I asked stupidly, the obvious hole in front of me.

"Jump in it. If you want to bury yourself, jump in!" He wasn't kidding. Usually, when I asked him what was wrong, he said, "Nothing." This was the closest to "something" he'd said. Quietly, I went inside.

I wanted to talk, to argue, but I couldn't. It was easier for me to ignore it. When I was growing up, I knew a couple in our neighborhood who never fought and never had cross words with each other. They would invite me over, and I noticed that when she did dishes, he walked by the sink and gave her backside a little pat. When he sat in his rocker at night, she gathered up her knitting, walked behind him, and rubbed his shoulder as she passed by.

I remember thinking, *This is love. They don't even fight. They love each other. When I get married, I want to be just like them. I don't want to fight, either. There's no reason for people to fight.* (I never saw them argue, so I figured they never did.) After that, whenever I had thoughts that approached anger, I figured there was something wrong with me. My friends didn't act angry; why couldn't I learn to control my feelings? I buried my anger and disagreements so deep that they wouldn't emerge until I'd been married twenty-three years.

I didn't mind being a good sport and doing things for Jim, but I wanted to hear that he knew I was doing a good job. "He doesn't appreciate me," I complained to my mother. She looked shocked.

"Don't tell me you're going to start having trouble," she said. "I always figured you two would be OK no matter what. Jim is so easygoing, so level-headed, so hard-working." Just what I needed to hear, I thought.

The one thing I did need to hear was that I had done a good job. I wanted Jim to say it, but he couldn't seem to. I never thought it was a selfish need of mine; I simply wanted to be told I was doing someone some good. When Mom pointed out to me what a great guy I married, I should have been glad, but I wanted sympathy.

Without conversation or communication, bits of problems grow into chunks of problems, and pieces of indecision enlarge until they become convincing insecurities. I let dark edges grow into our relationship. Jim was acting as he always had, and I was feeling, thinking, seeing, and knowing that things were not good. Whatever was wrong, I knew that I needed to change it.

I had an opportunity at a community dance. "Get your own ride home if you aren't ready now!" Jim said, walking away from me on the dance floor to get his coat. I stood there, trying to figure out what had made him so mad so fast. Then I knew—Joe and Marianne danced by and bumped us. I pushed Joe, and he pushed me back, laughing.

"If you want to monkey around, OK, but I'm leaving," Jim said. Jim didn't like a lot of nonsense in public. He had had enough of my silliness, as he saw it. If I wanted to go again, I would have to behave next time. I ran to the coatroom, got my jacket, and hurried after him. We lived only two miles out of town and I could have gotten a ride. (He didn't mean for me to, though.)

"I'm coming—wait!" I called after him. "Wait!"

When he got mad, I got mad. I couldn't say so, though, and that's as far as it went. I just wanted us to be loving partners. But somewhere along the way we began to own each other, and I didn't like it. Jim had no idea, though. Whenever we went somewhere I stuck close to him, because if I disappeared, he let me know about it later. "Where were you? I wanted to go home and you weren't around."

At first I made myself scarce so we wouldn't leave so early. Later I figured I might as well go home when he wanted to so it wouldn't be hard to get him to go the next time. I didn't admit to myself that his possessiveness was not a sign of love, and that my sticking close to him was not a way to show unity. United means being able to walk away, find conversation and friends, and return to each other to share what you want. It's up to both husband and wife, and it should be a happy decision.

Friends can be an important part of a marriage. When both partners enjoy each other's friends, it's nice. But it's not necessary. Each can have a different group of friends and still live together happily. There is only one firm, tough rule: friends have to be secondary. They cannot take precedence over a marriage relationship. I let that happen for a while.

When Jim and I couldn't talk, I talked to my friends. The trap occurred when they listened, took sides, and offered sympathy. "He was such a creep last night at the dance," I told Marianne. "Did you hear him tell me to get a ride home? He walked out and left me standing there. I felt like hitching a ride with someone else."

"You should have," she said. "He is a creep. He's got no right to let you feel that way. Lots of guys would have given you a ride home and been happy to do it."

As I listened to her, I felt fortified and important. I could stand up to him if he started that stuff again. Sympathy was the first thing I wanted, but the last thing I needed.

SOMETHING WORTH SAVING

Friends often mean the best for you, just as Marianne tried to help me. I ran to her with tales, stories, complaints, and ego trip reports; I used her to boost my own ego and never realized it. I talked to family, confiding my feelings of how unfair Jim was. They tried to be kind, and said they didn't realize he was like that. But they were trying to tell me they didn't believe me. I ignored them. I chose to listen to friends who fed me the lines I wanted to hear. But friends can divide couples, because problems can be magnified through others' eyes.

"You could have done so much better," Marianne remarked one day after listening to my complaints. Silently, I agreed. She bolstered my sour viewpoint.

While I talked to my friends, I didn't confide in Jim. Things that should have been shared between us were not. I made others a part of our marriage and left Jim out. That's another danger point, and a practice of many people. A husband can be a wife's best friend. Though he may answer her problems with, "Hmmm . . ." and "Well, what you should have done is . . . ," he's still the best one to talk to.

A wife should encourage her husband to take part in what he may consider her "silliness." She should ask him to go to Brownie Fly-ups, 4-H Award Nights, sixth-grade concerts, Honor Society inductions. Leaving him out is too easy. He needs the fun of watching the growth process of

But We Don't Have Any Problems

his children just as much as she does.

One of my friends listened to my problems with Jim, but wouldn't join in against him. "Have you tried prayer?" Ruth asked.

Sure, I thought sarcastically. *I'm going to pray about it. Everyone thinks praying about anything will fix it. Why don't they realize I'm miserable? How can I pray when I'm in this mood? Prayer is for church when it's quiet and the timing is right. Sure I'll pray about it—sure I will.*

"I don't think that's our answer," I stammered.

"God is the one you can always count on. He is your only true friend," she said. "If you feel alone, turn to him. You can turn to him for counsel, advice, discussion, and prayer. You'll learn to listen for his answers. They can be given in small ways, or they can hit you like a lightning bolt. But if you rely on him, you'll know you're not alone. While you're working on the marriage, or trying to find out what makes you tick, you'll know that—trite as it sounds—God is there."

I believe in God, I thought, *but I don't think he understands my frustration when I think no one cares.* I didn't think about the agonies God experienced when he saw Jesus on the cross, when he tried to talk to a people who wouldn't listen, when he tried to tell them of a love they could not grasp. I didn't think about the love that God has for me when I'm confused, mad, jealous, resentful, and selfish. I didn't think about the frustrations he feels every day, just watching people like me. I hadn't learned to lean on God. I just couldn't seem to rely on him. I was afraid to let my walls down and trust him.

These were just a few of the problems affecting me. I talked to friends, but not to Jim. I confided in others, but not in God. The problems just kept growing bigger.

SIX
The Lawyer

As I walked up the patterned red-brick sidewalk to the stately Victorian home that served as legal offices, I looked around nervously, hoping I wouldn't see anyone I knew. At the time I didn't know I'd be moving out in two months. I wasn't prepared for the events I would put into motion. June wedding, and twenty-three years later, July divorce.

Divorce. That was the last thing I wanted. No, that's not true; I did want a divorce. But I didn't want to be a divorced person. When I was growing up, divorce was scandalous.

"Divorced? She must have done something or he never would've left."

I recalled how some of my mother's friends referred to an acquaintance who had been married more than once: "She's been around, you know." A divorcee was a leper, her company not

SOMETHING WORTH SAVING

wanted by single or married adults. She would be after anyone's husband, boyfriend, neighbor; no one was safe. All of this was imprinted on my mind while I was growing up. Now I would be one of those talked about.

Times have changed, though. I've read that one out of two marriages today end in divorce. It's no longer possible not to know a divorced person. Communities have support groups for "parents without partners," singles, remarrieds. Stepfamilies have become so common that Ann Landers has published etiquette for the seating at weddings of step-families twice and thrice removed. People today are learning to deal with such situations, because whether we like it or not, they do exist.

Opening the eight-foot-tall, solid mahogany door, I expected a bong to sound. I had wanted the trip to make me feel safe and secure, not as if I were prying into Boris Karloff's private mansion.

I was two minutes early for the appointment and was told to wait in the lawyer's interior office. As I sat there, I felt more alone than at any time in my life, except when I was in labor with Diana and Jim was away in the navy. Nothing about the office accommodated how I felt. Nothing portrayed the despair that grabbed at my heart. Nothing revealed the violent vortex called divorce that seemed to be pulling me in. Everything there represented business as usual, right down to the desk calendar that showed the date. I thought it

The Lawyer

should have been at least a month behind, proving that time had stood still for someone else as it had for me. My life was a jumble inside my head, but this place was pure organization and logic.

The lawyer walked in, punctual to the minute, and seated himself in the oversized oak chair on wheels. He rolled it up to the desk opposite me.

"Whatcha need?" he asked, leaning back with his hands behind his head. "How can I help you get it?"

I wanted to tell him I didn't know. I had asked myself that question for the last five years. What did I need? Why wasn't my life with Jim—who was content to come home after work every day, eat dinner, watch TV, go to bed, and love me—enough? What was wrong with me? What *did* I need? What did I want?

"I guess I need a divorce. I want to be on my own."

It must have been someone else talking, I thought. Divorce? I had said the word out loud for the first time.

"You guess you need a divorce?" he mused. "You have to be more sure than that. You can't guess you need a divorce—either you know it or you don't."

I squirmed in my seat as he rolled his chair right up to the desk, looked me squarely in the eye, and spoke again. "You have a house? Think about that, how much it's worth. You own a car? Furniture?"

"I don't want anything except my clothes and what belongs to me."

I wanted out, that's all. I didn't want to do anything to make Jim work harder. He had worked hard enough already. We had gone a long way together, and he had worked during all of it.

"He hit you?" asked the lawyer, relaxing with his foot inside a pulled-out bottom desk drawer.

"No," I said, surprised that anyone would even think such a thing of Jim.

"He drink?"

"Of course not," I snapped, and thought of the beer that had sat in our refrigerator since last summer.

"He run around?"

"You've got to be kidding," I responded. "He'd rather be home than anywhere."

The lawyer threw his hands into the air with a final resolve. "Then what's the problem?" he asked, stymied.

How could I convey the loneliness I felt, the not-caring that seemed to permeate my marriage? How could I explain to him in the remaining three minutes that I could not continue my marriage as it was? How could I make him understand my feelings of mental and emotional singleness?

"He doesn't seem to care anymore, listen anymore, need me anymore."

I had come to this lawyer for fatherly advice, but he was only a few years older than our son. I wanted dependable counsel, the pipe-and-tweed-

The Lawyer

jacket type, not this harried youngster who continually looked at his watch, anticipating his next appointment.

"Well," he said, standing up, "the first visit is free. We'll talk about the fee on the next appointment, if you make one. Some of you women never come back." He ushered me out the door within the allotted fifteen minutes.

But I hadn't explained to this man the daily hurts that no one notices; I hadn't told him about the frustration I felt because I never received a single compliment. I hadn't made him see that a little praise from Jim would have worked wonders.

"What are you, a puppy?" Jim would say. "I have to pat you on the head and tell you you're doing a good job?"

I would shake my head and walk away, hating the thought of starting an argument. Why didn't I tell him, "Yes. I want to hear that. I need that. I want to know when I'm doing something right." Why couldn't I say that?

I would only be admitting I couldn't exist on my own if I let him know I enjoyed his approval. So I never let him know. When he answered me that way, I backed down; and I resented him for not giving me something that he didn't even realize I needed. So many times I had expected him to be a mind reader. How could I blame Jim when I had not told him? If I only hinted at what I wanted, what made me think that he would know what it was? Here was a man who spoke frankly, specifically, not in innuendos or hints, and I knew that. Why did I expect him to be different than he was?

My big lawyer confrontation was over, and I thought I hadn't handled it very well. The young man practically told me my problem wasn't serious. He didn't know that I planned to move out and that this was part of the procedure. He didn't realize my confusion. He didn't feel my despair. I felt bruises that didn't show. Mentally, I was a mess. Obviously, I wasn't one of the women he was used to representing. He had as much as said I wouldn't be back.

I knew the time would come when I would tell Jim I had talked to a lawyer. But Jim wouldn't like my telling someone else about our problems. To begin with, he thought we didn't have any.

"Everyone has problems," he had said. "You get too upset, that's all. You think everything is so serious. Why don't you relax once in awhile? It's not worth getting into a big, deep, dark discussion every time. When we need to talk, we'll talk. Right now, we don't have any problems." Sometimes he reconsidered: "Maybe you have problems, but I don't. If you think we need to go somewhere and talk to someone, why don't you go?" To Jim, everything would be OK tomorrow. Nothing was so bad that it required all the worrying I did.

These thoughts of a lifetime could not have

The Lawyer

been conveyed in a few short minutes to a lawyer I had never met before.

I had wanted a comforter, a shoulder to cry on, not a "hurry up and decide how much you want to get out of him" type of appointment. There was so much I wanted to share with someone who had a listening ear. Hearing the lawyer talk so clinically about Jim had upset me. Jim was nice. He was strong, stood up for what he believed in, worked hard, wasn't superficial.

But I needed more. I needed understanding and sensitivity. He needed dinner and the newspaper. He thought taking care of me was his most important job. To me, that meant talking and communicating; to him, it meant working hard five days a week, bringing home his paycheck, and handing it to me. Whenever I told him I had something on my mind, he would laugh and ask, "What'd you do, read another book today?"

As I got into the car to go back to work that July day, I knew I had to make a decision. No matter what excuses I made, what reasons I found, I knew I couldn't go on this way.

SEVEN
Packing

During the drive back to work, I concluded that I would solve my problems by escaping them. As my plan progressed logically in my head, I knew it all would work. Next week I would look at apartments. I wouldn't need much room, just something cute, cheerful, and cheap. After I found a place, I would put down a deposit—then move.

Through answering an ad in the newspaper, I met the realtor who would become my friend for my "alone" period. It felt strange telling someone else I planned to move out. Jim didn't even know.

Netta and I got to know each other in a close, personal, yet removed way. She didn't know where I lived or worked, but she had my telephone number at the office. I met her at her home to go apartment-hunting. I knew that her husband had suffered a severe heart attack a month before, in June, and that she had two

SOMETHING WORTH SAVING

children, three cats, and a dog. I never met her for lunch or coffee, and never had a private discussion with her. The personal knowledge she had of my life was not of an intimate nature, but of necessity. She respected my need for secrecy. It was a strange acquaintance, but it worked.

The first three apartments didn't make a hit with me: upstairs and crowded, downstairs and expensive, rundown and dirty. The second weekend I put down a deposit on a one-bedroom that looked better than the others I had seen.

"You could roller-skate in this kitchen!" Netta shouted, her enthusiasm echoing off the walls of the huge room. The refrigerator stood across the floor from the sink, and they were separated by at least ten feet. No stove. *That's OK*, I thought. *I'll get a hot plate. Like a garret in Greenwich Village. I'll go to garage sales and pick up what I need.*

I had made up my mind: I would move out. It was time to take care of myself. I was looking at life from my viewpoint, and I would take care of me first.

Back home, I cleaned out everything with a new attitude. Sort out, clean, pack some things and kiss some good-bye: dishes that meant something to me, Christmas presents from friends, doilies from deceased aunts and grandmothers, precious embroidered pillowcases. I couldn't fit all these things.

I had saved the kids' grade-school treasures for

Packing

almost twenty years. There was a handprint in hardened plaster of a small kindergarten-sized hand, painted for a long-ago Mother's Day, and the silhouette of our only son, paraded home proudly from the first grade years ago. I remembered that year. It was a special time. Joe was going to be seven, and was very excited.

"This is your 'special guest' year for your birthday party," I reminded him. "Decide on one friend you want to come and let me know, so I can invite him."

"Can I invite my friend instead?"

"Sure," I said, grateful that the small detail would not be at the mercy of my slippery memory.

For the night of his birthday, I fixed his favorite: chocolate cake, chocolate frosting, and chocolate decorations. With dinner ready, I still didn't see any special friend's mother turning into the driveway. Maybe Joe forgot to invite one. Then I heard the knock at the door.

"Open the door and let your little friend in," I coaxed.

Joe ran to the door, opening it for a tall woman, beautifully coiffed, a white-haired picture of grace—our son's seventy-year-old first-grade teacher.

"Miss 'Larkey! Miss 'Larkey!" he yelled, jumping up and down. He took her by the hand and led her down the hallway and into the dining room. "You're just in time. We're gonna eat now." We all sat down to a very special dinner with this extremely special guest.

I had gotten sidetracked. I sat down on the floor and found more special remembrances I had saved through the years. One was a poem, glued painstakingly but crookedly onto black paper under a gold, pasted-on leaf. Denise's printing had been a little askew, running down the paper as if the words would slide off the bottom. It reminded me of a particular note she once found.

She had come home from second grade early that day; I was still shopping for groceries. The fuel oil delivery man had left a tank of oil and poked the bill inside the screen to the back door. Not being able to read it, Denise had inspected the pink, official-looking paper and surmised it to be a note from her mother and father. She crossed two busy highways to get to the neighborhood store where I was shopping. I was shocked to see her, and asked, amid scolding, what she was thinking of, walking across the high-traffic road after we had told her not to.

"I saw your note on the door," she said. "I knew *what* it said." Though she could not read, her penchant for melodrama supplied the details. "You were gone and never coming back." (You would have thought we abandoned this child at regular intervals.) She was not so heartbroken, though, that she didn't have the presence of mind

Packing

to select a small doll while at the store, charging it to an account I did not have. (She returned the doll, at my insistence, with apologies to the storekeeper.)

Basking in the memories, I took one such treasure of each child, and left the rest for Jim. I pulled out the large wooden chest of Christmas decorations. I couldn't leave my decorations; Christmas was special to our whole family. We had made lots of things to hang on the tree.

I began to sort out ornaments that were special to me.

What are these little lace gloves doing in the Christmas ornaments? Sarah was three the year she had gotten them from her grandmother. Sarah loved to dress up "pretty." She insisted on wearing her new gift from Grandma to a mother-daughter banquet at church. It was a chore for her to pull each tiny finger into each white finger of the tiny glove, one by one. The lacy gloves wrinkled but Sarah patiently worked, a finger at a time, until one whole hand was dressed. The other hand was even more difficult. With one glove on, her other hand looked as if it were destined to be bare for the evening.

I helped her—finger by finger, smoothing the soft silky material over the little knuckles, working lacy fingers up and over. Finally, she was ready! Sarah held her small hands up to the light as if to look through them, and checked during a lengthy procedure for any errors in quality or taste.

SOMETHING WORTH SAVING

I was very proud as I sat at the table with my three daughters. Sarah was proud, too—of her gloves. She held her gloved fingers up as if letting her nails dry, waving them back and forth over the plate.

"Take off your gloves, honey," I urged.

"No."

"You can't eat with them on. You'll get them dirty."

"No, I won't."

"Let me help you."

"No, I need to leave them on. They're too hard to work." That made sense to me. She left the gloves on, and ate her dinner in elegance.

She had packed her special gift in my wooden box of Christmas decorations, a very special place. In it were other ornaments dear to me, things from friends and from family. I carefully packed and marked all the boxes, and now I would set them apart, marked Take and Leave. Jim wouldn't pry into my things; he respected my privacy. He would never know about my Christmas boxes. It was hard deciding which family mementos to pack up and move later, and which to leave behind for Jim. But I did it. I felt more organized and orderly.

Photographs had to be separated. I had gone through the family albums, extra scrapbooks, and tin boxes of pictures.

I held up a picture that must have been taken in Canada—the rain, the sweatshirts. It had been

Packing

chilly for July. I wished I had the camera when the kids rushed into the swimming area with goose pimples and chattering teeth. The weather was sunny and pretty, but the water was cold. Clouds covered the swimming area, and everything got dark. Snowflakes fell, tiny and minute, but snowflakes nonetheless. The kids laughed at the idea of swimming while it snowed. Jim and I made hot chocolate over the campfire for when the kids came out of the water, "freezing to def," as they said.

I had saved pictures of weddings, picnics, and reunions. My in-laws had included me in family fun, especially when Jim was away in the navy. His mom and dad welcomed me and introduced me to everyone at their family reunion. Cousins and aunts and uncles gathered around to smile and see whom Jim had gotten hooked up with. Everyone was friendly, so I wasn't too scared. But they were a lot of people to meet at one time. I had fed Diana her baby food and situated her in the swing, which hung on a spring hook in the dining room doorway. She watched the proceedings and felt at home being the center of attention. Traffic streamed past her from the table to the refrigerator to the sink. She talked to the ceiling, the chairs, and occasionally a cousin or two.

Jim's Uncle Andy had the biggest family there: fourteen children so far. Aunt Georgia had control of the offspring most of the time. She had trained each child to watch after the next in line.

SOMETHING WORTH SAVING

When the time came to go home, Georgia gave roundup instructions.

From young adults to babies, children were picked up, packed up, and directed toward the car. They all waved and chattered happily, talking about next year's reunion and the possibility of reserving a pavilion in the state park so we could all be inside if it rained.

I looked toward the dining room. The swing was empty! I saw no sign of Diana anywhere. I checked the living room and the laps of every grandmother and aunt sitting there. No Diana. I looked outside, wondering where a baby who could not walk would have gone. I saw Uncle Andy and Aunt Georgia's car in the driveway, starting up and slowly rolling in reverse, the windows filled with children waving to aunts, cousins, and friends.

A familiar face smiled at me from the backseat. Diana! They had picked her up and put her in their car.

"Wait!" I yelled. "You've got mine!" They looked at me as if I had lost a marble or two. "Wait! Diana is in the backseat! You've got so many—she's the only one I've got! *Wait!*" I yelled even louder, running until I caught up with their car as it pulled onto the road.

Finally, they realized what I was saying and stopped the car. One of the young brothers had scooped up Diana, wrapped her snugly in her

Packing

blanket and put her in the car with the rest of his siblings. Their family usually had a baby that size, so he figured Diana must be theirs. Uncle Andy gave me back my only child. "Seems like the kids got us one too many." He looked with amusement at me, the nervous young newcomer to the clan. They joked about that incident each year.

I continued through the photographs of kindergarten graduations, sixth-grade concerts, National Honor Society inductions. I remembered many things about the kids and the things they said, activities we planned together, nights I went to school alone to watch them perform. ("Mothers do those things better," Jim had said. "You can tell me about it when you get back." But I wanted him there. The kids wanted him there. He would do anything for them, but, as he saw it, it wasn't necessary to be a school-function parent.)

I tried to decide which snapshots to leave. There were pictures of proms, new cars, cheerleading, acrobatics, basketball jump shots. Jim should have his own file of his kids' activities, I thought. There were more memories here than I wanted to leave behind. I meticulously sorted and set aside an envelope of photos for each child. I also put aside one for me; it would have to do. I continued until I had what I considered necessary for "starting over." Two boxes. Not much to show for all those years.

I knew I wouldn't be around to eat the pickles

SOMETHING WORTH SAVING

I had canned. I realized someone else would have to tell Jim how to fix the frozen beans.

I had heard of some friends' anniversary celebration and didn't know whether I would be around to attend. Birthdays would no longer be fun to anticipate. I was sure our friends would not invite me after I ducked out.

Begin again. I knew I had to. It was important to be married to a close friend. I had mentioned that before, in the form of advice to our four now-grown children. "Do whatever you feel you need to do to make yourself happy. You can't live your life for someone else. Be happy." No one told me to leave. No one told me not to. No guilt trips, no judgment, just decide for yourself.

It would be hard, but only for a while. I had to continue with my plan.

As I walked through the house, thinking consumed most of my time. I was a bomb waiting to explode. Where would I be next Christmas? I thought. Who would spend it with me? Would I ever have my own "things" again? Would I cultivate new friendships? Would I grow into one of those unhappy, bitter, resentful, divorced women I knew? Would I be able to make it on my salary?

I had always needed others, and liked close relationships. Would I have to settle for less now? I wondered.

The big step I was considering required time to stop and think. But I had stopped and thought and wondered. I wondered and wondered some

Packing

more. No one else could tell me what to do, I knew that. Leaving was something I had to decide on, figure out, and do for myself.

Once I was alone, I could get it together. I could solve everything then.

EIGHT
Moving Back

The leaves were beginning to turn colors and drop off. It was beautiful September weather. I took long walks on the hill, enjoying the dry crush and crackle where I stepped. I was home. Things weren't perfect, but I was home. I had stayed away from this place only one night, two months earlier. And in the two short months since my return, our marriage had changed.

I had kept the apartment all that time. I knew, in the back of my mind, that it would be there for me in case things didn't work out. In case we started arguing again. In case I still felt I had to be alone.

One Saturday, however, I realized it was unfair to hold that possibility over Jim's head any longer. He couldn't relax until I let the apartment go. I was not allowing him to feel any stability or commitment from me. I expected him to do this, do that for me and in return, I did nothing. It took those two months for me to see how selfish I was being. I had wanted to be sure, to not take any chances. Love is not like that, though. As Jim and I continued to talk during that time, I saw how I had exploited the new give-and-take we had established and used it to my advantage.

I called Netta and told her I would be moving my things out by the end of the month.

"Is it better?" she asked.

"I think so," I hedged.

"Maybe this bought you the time you needed, to think things over?" she asked, but she saw all along that I had been mixed up, unsure. I had told her about the old days Jim and I had, so she knew there was a reason I should care about him. She knew even before I did that I cared. She later told me I knew these things, but I didn't admit them to myself.

I had a final retreat, one more night at the apartment after my late-night economics course on Wednesday. Walking into the kitchen after class, I noticed how different it looked. On that first night two months ago, it had been my new home. Now it was no one's.

My things were still there—clothes, a few pairs of shoes, the bed, nightstand, sewing machine, a chair, and my double-keyboard organ—all inanimate objects sitting there, with no care or purpose given to them. Layers of dust showed the neglect. Things are just things without people to care

Moving Back

about them. People are, too. They have to care about themselves and each other. Then they're real.

I looked over the small collection of objects I had thought so important, things I felt *had* to be included in my new life. What were they worth in dollars? Not much, to begin again. Not much, to take away from twenty-three years of marriage. Not much to feel that I, who had to start over, was real. Without me here to care for them, they were nothing but things. I guess I didn't really care about them after all. I had lived two months without them and survived.

Moving them back would be an act of my love for Jim. I wasn't sure yet of everything we needed to do to be happy, but I wanted to let him know I would try. It was the end of an era for me. I walked through the echoing rooms putting my towels, dishes, and canned goods back into the boxes I had left on the floor—years ago, it seemed. I wanted to come here alone and to get things ready. I should, I thought. When Jim would come on Saturday, it should be all done, ready to move out. At least he wouldn't have to pack it all up.

Jim, our son-in-law, Joe, and I rode to the apartment in the truck on Saturday. The ride was quiet. Joe made small talk, happy that I was officially coming home. I was getting better acquainted with this man who had married our oldest daughter. I liked him more all the time.

"They're building a new barn," he said, pointing out our neighbors' industrious construction. "Sure is cold today for September. Wonder if they're ever going to cut that hay. Been ready for a month now." His talk wasn't directed at anyone, but it filled the silence.

Jim must have been thinking about us, how we would continue from here. I don't know exactly what he was thinking, and he didn't say, of course. He just kept driving. I rode along listening to Joe, glad he was so happy. We had our days of doubts about him. He and Diana were in love so young. She was fourteen, and they wanted to be together more than anything. Jim didn't want her to date, but I wasn't sure, and Diana could tell we were not in agreement. We blamed Joe for a long time, finally realizing it was not all his fault.

Eventually, they decided they had to be together, and Diana left home when she was fifteen and a half. I agonized over the leaving of our eldest daughter. Jim and I couldn't talk about it. He didn't approve and couldn't discuss it. I didn't approve but needed to share my hurt feelings. The division between us grew.

Joe and Diana got married on the top of a hill a year and a half later, on a breezy, sunny day. I went to the wedding to regain my daughter; Jim stayed away. He didn't want any part of Diana and Joe, after the way they had handled their lives. I wanted to see them, but it caused too many problems with Jim, so I kept my distance. Jim and I

Moving Back

had had many plans for Diana, and she had bypassed every one.

The first few months were hard. They didn't need us—they had each other. But I wanted them to be part of our lives. Diana loved deeply, us *and* Joe, and Jim and I were divided, between each other and our love for her. Then came that special birthday of mine, one of the many times I loved Jim so much.

"We're going up to Mom's for dinner," he said. "Get ready, because we'll leave a little early." My birthdays weren't usually a big deal to Jim, and I was glad that he remembered. We were doing something together, and he was taking charge. It would be fun to get away.

We lived only fifteen miles from his mom and dad, and up the road we went as usual until Jim took a wrong turn. "You taking a shortcut I don't know about?" I asked, but he looked straight ahead, not answering. The only person I knew who lived on this road was . . . Diana. But he had not talked to her for over a year. "Where are we going?" I asked, more insistent than at first. Still no answer.

As he pulled into Diana and Joe's driveway, he turned to me and smiled. "Happy birthday." Diana stepped out of the trailer, pulling her jacket around her shoulders and carrying our grandchild. She was smiling. Jim was smiling.

I had seen the baby only one other time—when Diana had called me nervously right after

Erika was born. "Can you come up and show me how to give her a bath?" I went to help. The love we each had for the new baby melted some of the tension, but we hadn't known how to bridge the gap.

I watched Diana approach the car, and loved Jim for this birthday surprise. They smiled and I cried. (I always cried.) Joe was working and couldn't join us for dinner, Diana told me, but she would be with me on that special birthday.

The three of us became close all over again. Jim and I enjoyed watching our firstborn assume the role of mother, and she became part of us once more. Joe was not as easily moved into the center of the group. Jim had seen him as an enemy: he was the culprit who stole our baby. He didn't say much, but we all tried to be civil, to be a family.

The more I knew Joe, the more I realized he was like us. He loved Diana as much as we did. He seemed so different—the long hair, the beard, and the fast car when he had been a few years younger; we dared not trust our daughter to him. He got her anyway. Now we needed to mend the wounds and fix the hurts, so we tried.

Joe wanted to be family too, but he didn't know us, and thus didn't know how. He did his own quiet things: repairing our car, working around outside, being busy, and working hard at his job for his own family. We began to notice what a nice guy he was. Under the hair and the quiet demeanor, he was nice to know. His

Moving Back

strength ran silent but deep, and I knew this from the way he volunteered to help Jim move my things back. He didn't want Jim to be alone.

Jim and Joe walked into my short-term home away from home. We walked from room to room, seeing my things stuffed into boxes. Jim shook his head. "Funny, seeing your stuff here, not at home where it belongs. Gives me the creeps." He walked ahead, wanting to be alone with his thoughts. I let him walk.

We moved the boxes into the back of the truck without a word. It was hard to know what to say. I had moved out alone in silence. I was moving back home, too, in silence. Joe made the snappy patter needed to lighten up the situation.

"You sure do have a lot of shoes. . . . Wow, look at this—never saw you wear this before." His added humor sounded like Netta's: "You need roller skates to get around this kitchen."

We got everything in the back of the pickup and headed out. I left the key inside. The final looking around—checking the pantry, the bathroom medicine cabinet—I did by myself. I closed the door knowing I would not be back. This so-called freedom was not for me, I discovered. I liked being married, having a person to come home to. Liked having one come home to me. The apartment had served a purpose for me. I had left to remove myself from what I thought was an unsolvable problem. If I couldn't fix it, I thought, I would get away from it.

SOMETHING WORTH SAVING

Now there was no need to get away. Jim and I were talking at last. We were going to solve it. I had given up on us, but Jim never did. We were going home.

NINE
Making It Work

We relaxed and got used to the idea of being together again, and for the first time we consciously began to put the other person's wants and needs first. We talked. We got inside each other's minds, thoughts, hurts, and joys. This closeness was what I had always wanted, and finally we had it. We left the TV off when we got home from work, and we talked. We kept it turned off and ate dinner. We kept it turned off still and made love. I enjoyed Jim's undivided attention and wanted even more.

I received flowers from him. Yellow mums for my birthday, a rose for Sunday, dried arrangements for Halloween. When I got home from work, they were on the table. When I got home from class, they were there. When I got the mail there were cards from him. This was a new man, and I was loving all of it.

The closeness we began to develop led to even more caring, and in the new communication we had, I learned more about Jim than I had ever known or paid attention to. He asked me about my thoughts, and he listened. I asked about his ideas, and I listened.

Once we started these talks, I began to realize many things. For years I had been annoyed by some of his gestures, like the hugs from behind at the sink. How I had wanted to let him know that I hated having him come up behind me, do whatever he was enamored to do, then walk away to watch TV, leaving me there with my hands in hot, soapy water. It was an unthinking gesture, one that suggested I wasn't really there, that I was just something for him to hug, feel, or touch. No word or comment from him; just a touch and he was gone. I hated it, but he never knew it—because I never told him.

When we talked, I mentioned these repeated encounters and my anger that the kitchen sink was not the place for that. Jim was amazed. He said he couldn't figure out why I was so mad; he simply had needed to touch me before going back to what he'd been doing. He didn't think it was necessary to say much to me, because I was busy. In my opinion it was like a break in the action, a commercial.

Just discussing it made a difference. He had no idea how much I hated it. If he had waited until I

Making It Work

could respond by hugging him or kissing him back, I would have felt that I mattered. He thought about me so much, he said, that it was a way of "touching base" while we were both home and busy.

After I expressed my feelings, Jim didn't think he should hug or kiss me at all, and he stopped altogether. He had misinterpreted my complaint, and thought I hated love or sex or loving. We had to start over. I had to let him know that it wasn't the act but the method that seemed to deny my feelings in the matter. I loved to be loved, but I wanted to be included in the act. We talked some more. Again, he didn't realize I felt that way. But how could he, when I never told him?

We tiptoed around one another as if it were naptime in the nursery. We tried to be quiet, being oh-so-careful not to be a problem to each other while busy, sleeping, reading the paper, or watching TV. We wanted to make it work. But if you try too hard to make something work, it does not work.

Some people just don't fit into certain molds, even if they try. It's like the round peg in the square hole. You get out the hammer, try to force it by whacking it a few times, and it still won't fit. The only way to make it fit is by whittling off a little of the sides. When you whittle off enough, the peg is not round anymore. It fits into a square hole, but did I really want the round peg to be square? Was I happier having Jim be himself, or whittling him away into someone else? I began to ask myself.

I noticed the lines and the tightness around his face. He looked nervous, as though he was under some kind of stress.

"You don't have to buy me flowers and presents for every occasion, you know," I told him. "It's not required."

He looked at me, with an expression of genuine surprise. "I thought that's one of the things you'd been wanting. How am I supposed to know what you want?"

He thought he finally had the right combination and I had changed again. I had programmed him into being the caring, suburban, phony husband I thought I wanted, and now that I had him performing to my order, I didn't like it. He was more confused than ever. I had never wanted a man like that.

One of the reasons I enjoyed Jim was that what he said and meant were the same. He was not superficial, and I began to appreciate that. When you're married to an honest man, you have difficult days, but at least you know why. I was beginning to learn a lot of things about this man—mainly, that I liked him better the old way. He had been going through life on his own course, not worrying about much, before I convinced him how unhappy I was. When he tried to change I still wasn't happy. He gave up.

Making It Work

"It doesn't matter what I do," he reasoned. "It won't be right to you."

The flowers and gifts stopped. He didn't care what I did, he said; he couldn't stop me anyway. I soon discovered that along with this carefree attitude came a robot: No matter what I said, it was OK with Jim. If I wanted to go bowling, out to dinner, to class, to choir, to a rendezvous in Timbuktu, no problem. I had deprogrammed him into another type of programmed machine. "Do what makes you happy," he said. (What he meant was, "I'm not sure what it is, so I'll back out of the way.") He surrendered to the final act of our marriage, and expected the curtain to close. It seemed to him that there was no hope.

It was then that I began to see what I had done to him. I had been looking for approval, love, or "strokes," as they call them in psychologists' circles. I had depended on him to give me all those things, but it wasn't possible. I couldn't get self-worth from others. No one could give me that but me.

Saturday mornings were good times for us to talk. One Saturday, however, our talking led to an argument. We fought.

"Get out," Jim said. "I don't need this. Don't take anything this time. Just leave." He was tired of being my understanding roommate for the past few months, fed up with my indecision, my frustration, and my confusion. He didn't understand any of it. He couldn't figure out what was bugging

SOMETHING WORTH SAVING

me, and thought I had gone off the deep end. I couldn't put it into logical explanation, and I thought, *Maybe I am crazy.*

After those initial, blissful weeks of my being home, we had talked and discussed and argued, and I closed my ears. I didn't want this—a debate every weekend.

"Say it. I'm wrong," Jim challenged that particular Saturday. "Why don't you say it? Why do you always back off?"

I couldn't explain it. Every time an argument started, I felt sick in the pit of my stomach. I hated to argue. If I could escape it, I did. This time, leaving was my escape. I grabbed my jacket and stormed out to the porch to get away from the arguing. He locked the door and sat down in his chair with his back to me. I could see him through the window. OK, I complained to the icy morning air, *if he wants me to leave, I'll go.* I walked out to the car and got in. I tried to start it, but it wouldn't turn over.

I saw Jim come out of the basement door, madder than ever and yelling something. I locked the car doors and rolled up the windows as fast as I could. I wasn't afraid of the Jim I'd married, but this was not he. He picked up a log from the woodpile and threatened to throw it at the car window, menacingly. I kept trying the starter, and it caught. I put the car in reverse and backed out hurriedly, all the way to the road.

I was sweating profusely in the middle of a

Making It Work

northeast winter. The hairs on my neck were standing up, stiff and chilled. Jim stood near the house, the log still in his hand. He was yelling and shaking his fist at an imaginary enemy. He looked hateful. But when I looked back and saw this man with whom I had loved and lived, I shifted into gear and drove back up our long, sloping driveway. I didn't seem to have a thought about what I was doing—no time to wonder what and why. Someone else had my foot on the pedal, my hands on the wheel.

When I stopped the car next to him, he snarled, "What'd you forget?"

"You," I said.

There were many times like that. I would want to go; he would tell me to go. I would go; I would come back. Sometimes I didn't get as far as the car, and except for the time I moved out two months before, I never got farther than the driveway. The solution always eluded us. We both cared, there was no doubting that. But when we tried to make things work, we resented, fought, hurt, and yelled. In the end, I always wanted to leave.

You can do it, I told myself. *You can stick this out. There's never been a divorce in your family. Make this work. Hang in there.* I tried harder, but trying something daily is very tiring.

Friends would ask, "How're you two doing? Working it out?" When people ask a blunt question, point-blank, it's hard to lie. The family asked, "You OK? Things better?" and I'd smile and nod. But things weren't better.

Whatever people need to do to make things better, Jim and I didn't know. I was determined to make it work; Jim, on the other hand, reasoned according to his day-to-day acceptance of life that our marriage simply would work out or it wouldn't. He didn't understand the whole conflict to begin with. He figured it was my "time of life" or "empty-nest," or "monthly blues," or something. He couldn't believe my confusion was real.

Make it work, we thought—that's what we both had decided to do, regardless of our differing philosophies. We would, by God, make it work.

It should not have surprised me that it didn't work.

Trust is a fragile thing. Though it can withstand all hazards of nature and the universe, trust can be destroyed by a look, a touch, a word. So much hinges on this mystery of learning to count on someone else.

I had both counted on Jim and taken him for granted. He had done the same. Without giving me all the candy coating I thought I needed, he had taken me for granted and relied on me, and I had shaken his trust. He wasn't sure what I wanted anymore, what I needed from him, or even who I was. Trust cannot survive all that. Love might endure, but trust can crack and never be the same.

Making It Work

I had an expression that meant "no trust" to me: "The walls go up," I'd say. I couldn't live with my walls up. If I didn't trust someone, I wouldn't let that person inside the walls. People put up walls every day, and refuse to let others in. Trust is the intangible thing that allows us to be unafraid, to let someone get within the walls.

But when trust is abused as if it means nothing, the walls go up with double reinforcements. Double walls are harder to take down than any other kind. Hardly anyone is willing to take a chance on a second hurt.

Jim was unsure what had happened in those few months and why. He had given trust and it had been stepped on, and now he began to put up walls. Love can climb over walls, but not easily. Mistrust is like the quiet fog that creeps over a town at night: You don't hear it, and you're not looking for it so you don't see it . . . but it comes, and in the morning you can't see anything else.

By leaving, I had undone things that neither of us could fix. The trust had been delicately shaken. After that, it was different . . . and staying together wasn't easy.

TEN
Women Who Left, Women Who Stayed

I have many friends who are unhappy with their marital status. Some of them are divorced, and some of them are married. Relationships don't seem to carry any guarantees.

Before I moved out for the first time, I talked to my friend Jean about my own problems. "I want to get out for good," I said, "but I don't know when would be a good time." I'd related our daily barbs, the unsaid, unfriendly feelings. Jean sympathized and listened.

Then she told me it was that way at her house too. "We don't have anything in common but our daughter, Mandy," she said. "I don't like to go out drinking the way Bill does. For him, life is nothing but a lavish list of parties. If he can find fault with me in front of our friends, he's ecstatic. He'll make any cutting remark he can think of and make a big deal out of it. They say you'll know the right time to leave, and when it's time, you just go. That's what they say, anyway."

One Monday, I came to work and saw Jean at the coffee machine. She looked happy, silly, and even a little nervous.

"What's with you?" I asked.

"I moved out over the weekend," she said in a whisper. "I feel better than I have in months. I don't have to answer to anyone or apologize every time I say something I feel like saying. I don't have to play the dumb wife anymore. You know what I found out? I'm smart! I just never dared to show it before!"

"I didn't know you were thinking about moving out," I said. She had never mentioned it. Whenever we talked, it was about when I would know the right time.

"When it's time, you just do it, like we talked about," said Jean. "I saw an apartment on Saturday and it was empty, so the landlady said I could move right in. I thought about waiting, but figured, why not now? I was tired of his mouth. The verbal abuse was more than I needed. He didn't really care about me. He was too busy worrying about himself."

Jim and I had problems communicating, but I didn't have half the problems Jean did. I knew Bill. He was famous for his cruel speeches, and made fun of Jean anytime he got an audience. Everyone got tired of it, but that didn't stop him. I was glad I didn't have a husband like him.

Women Who Left, Women Who Stayed

Evelyn was another good friend. I would tell her how confused I was and she would answer with reasons why I should understand Jim better. She had a way of taking the other side, like a debater. She worked hard on me, trying to help me think out every angle and realize the finality of what I was considering. "Don't make a move you'll be sorry for," she advised. "Don't take a step you can't retrace."

I appreciated her help, but I thought she couldn't understand my loneliness. Then I found out differently.

"I left once," she said. "I was doing OK, but he wouldn't let me take the kids with me. We went to court. It got nasty. Neither one of us would give in, so the judge decided, since they were teenagers, they could decide where they wanted to live. I couldn't put them through that . . . so I went back home. I'm sorry I did it—the whole thing. He loves to rub it in."

Evelyn cared about people, and needed to know someone cared about her. But she couldn't get her husband to come off his high horse. He acted as though he had never made a mistake, and had a real chip on his shoulder. I never could figure out why he wanted her back. He acted as if he hated her more than her loved her.

Tammy was the petite, dainty mother of four energetic boys. Her husband was a dentist, much older than she.

"How're you doing?" she asked one day at

lunch, one of many I had shared with her. She was a listener who never told me how things were with her. She was uptight and nervous. Unhappy people have a way of knowing when others are unhappy, and I knew she was. I wished I could reach out to her, but I didn't know what she needed.

It could have been their age difference, her need for tenderness, her loneliness when he played golf each weekend, his drinking to excess—any one of these things. But she had never complained to me. As good a listener as she was, she never learned how to confide in others or to share herself.

One day she was quieter than usual. "Everything OK?" I asked.

"No," she replied. "What's the matter with me? I've got everything a woman could want, yet I want more."

"Does your husband know you're unhappy?"

"No. We never talk about personal things like that. He gets too upset."

Stacey was a friend who had been married twenty-seven years. She met me one day for lunch and seemed preoccupied. She gave me a surface smile, and bantered on about the kids, school functions, and how her husband's job was going. I knew she had more on her mind when she called me about lunch; her voice had sounded strained. I thought she was about to explode as she tapped her fingers on the edge of the table.

Her eyes looked sad. She picked up her fork and poked at her food. I listened until she finished sharing her mundane news. Finally, I couldn't stand her act any longer.

"Something wrong?" The question jumped out of my mouth, point-blank.

Her eyes welled over with tears. "I don't know what to do," she said. "I want to be a good, loving wife. But nothing I ever do is right. He criticizes me all the time. When he's working, he's happy. When he's home, he complains. I try to do what I think he wants, but I'm nervous all the time. I don't please him."

In her quest for approval, Stacey was involved with a man who went to her church. She saw him every week. She was vulnerable, ripe for another person to let her know she was loved and appreciated. She needed to know she was loved more than she needed anything else.

Guilt had been eating her alive. Although she was a Christian, she was involved with a married man, and it was tearing her apart. She knew God's people were not supposed to do anything like that.

"I know God realizes I'm human," she said. "But how do I get out from under the terrible pressure of sin? Even if God forgives me, I'm not sure I can forgive myself. At this point, I don't know if I can let go of this relationship. It gives me a kind of security, knowing someone cares."

It's too bad she wasn't around when I talked

to Martha, an older and wiser friend who lived nearby and had tried to help me. Martha used to annoy me because she had answers for every situation. "When you're working only to please someone else," she said, "you never will. When you go against what you believe to convince someone you feel the same way they do, you lose. You have to be true to yourself—to God's plan for you, to be real and honest. The agony you feel when you deny that truth is like the frustration God feels for you." Martha had a way of making me listen.

I remembered more of what she had said: "Each of us needs to know how special we are. To feel loved and appreciated, we must first love and appreciate ourselves, as the Lord does. It's incomprehensible, unfathomable, to grasp the depth of love he has for us. If we try to understand his love, we can take anything to him, and life becomes better.

"When I realized I mattered to God," Martha had confided, "I began to matter to me. Up until then, I had been looking to get all my 'strokes' from others. No one else can do that for you but God. When I relied on someone else to make me feel important, I set myself up to be hurt."

Martha had been through plenty, I surmised. Her husband divorced her after hearing about Martha's friendship with her boss. She thought her life would be happier if she got away from her husband. By the time she realized how important her husband and her home were to her, she had lost them both. She attained her wisdom after a painful process of discovery which occurred too late to save her own marriage. Now Martha tried to help others save theirs.

Martha's years of experience educated me even more over coffee one day. "Marriage is a way of showing each other love, friendship, compassion, and caring. It shouldn't be a way of depending on each other for approval. When you do that, you put the other person in charge. You have to know that you're OK before you can give to others. You'll never find your self-esteem in someone else. Once you know, inside, that you're OK, then you're OK.

"It's like credit," she continued. "You have to have it to get it. As trite as it sounds, if you rely on God, you learn that you are OK. You matter. You don't have to look to other people to convince you of that. I discovered that when I wanted to go back to my husband, he didn't want me. I was lost, had no one. Finally I figured out the only one I could count on was God. So I prayed and asked him for help."

Each friend had had a unique marriage. Each one thought her relationship had been the only one of its kind in history. Each one had handled her situation differently.

Jean is remarried now. In the four years she was single, she was lonely. She wished she and Bill could have worked out their problems—that she could have stayed. But there was no way. They were at opposite ends of the spectrum. She wanted one thing, he another. Talking might have helped, if he had learned to listen and care about her. Financially, Jean started over. Working extra hours and begging for past-due support payments was the only way she could make it work. She didn't think leaving was her best choice; she thought it was her only choice.

Evelyn stays home, working part time. She's not happy, and condemns herself for leaving and even more so for going back. She's still confused. She wishes she could find a way to care about her husband. She remembers how alone she felt after she moved out, and doesn't want to feel that way again. She would rather be home with her kids than alone anywhere else. Her husband never misses a chance to remind her of her stupidity. She's trapped in a daily hassle of harassment.

Tammy is at home—in limbo. She never let loose, and hasn't been happy since our talk. If she could release her attitudes and feelings, maybe she could find the love and approval she needs within herself. I think what she's looking for is there.

Stacey is searching. Her heart is torn; she knows that what she's doing is wrong. She's caught up in feeling unloved, yet needing to be loved.

We all know people with problems—men and women who stay together because of their children, people who stay married because guilt does not permit them to divorce. When I think about Martha's incisive wisdom, I realize that these are not reasons to stay married. But divorce is not always the answer; it doesn't offer any better guarantees than marriage. It is a last resort for some people. Faced with physical or verbal abuse, or a tormenting mental cruelty, many wives decide they've had enough.

For the rest of us, is it possible to head off divorce? If the solution is in communication, can we erase mistrust and eradicate doubt when we exchange ideas? Isn't it worth trying to find out? Isn't it worth trying? I never had to worry about abuse of any kind from Jim. In fact, I had taken his protective nature for granted. The one thing I always counted on was Jim's concern for me, even though it sometimes came in the form of anger.

"God's people make mistakes, too," I told Stacey, repeating Martha's words. "God loves you anyway. He hates to see you hurting. It hurts him when you hurt."

"I'll have to bring myself out of this, won't I?" she had asked.

"Not by yourself." I had known that God would take care of her through prayer, and that it would be difficult for her, but not impossible.

God seemed to be talking to me, too. The more I listened and counseled my friends, the more I understood about myself. Why couldn't I hear the words I spoke to Stacey? Why wouldn't I take my own advice?

I had been away from God in thought. I had been trying to do it all. Maybe it was time for me to ask for his help. I had to give it a try.

ELEVEN
I Started to Pray

"Pray about it," my friend Ruth once said.

"Oh sure," I whined. "With all the fighting and arguing, who can pray?"

I had attended church for over forty years, had heard members pray there, and had recited the Lord's Prayer with them. I knew that God was there. I knew that he loved me, and I knew that he was my friend. Still, he was way . . . up . . . *there*. I knew he was there because that's where I left him. I never called on him to help me—I thought he would love me more if I helped him all I could. I thought he expected me to take care of myself. But I became so frustrated inside, so resentful, that I started to pray:

"Lord, you know how Jim and I are. We don't talk to each other. We don't know each other. Please, Lord, if there's a way you can help me, do it. Get me away from here so I can find a solution. Help me fix up my life."

That was in late November, on a cold, snowy night. The next morning at work I made some sales calls, one to a regular customer of mine.

"It's cold here," I said. "Our winter is only beginning. We've got until May before we'll see the grass again."

"You should come out west and work for me," he said. *Did I hear right? Yes.* "You should come out here and live in our sunshine. Work for me," he repeated. I had goose pimples, chills—an answer to prayer! Maybe God did want me to go, to do my own thing. I told my generous client I would talk to him when he was more serious, and hung up.

At home, I couldn't get his suggestion off my mind. This really was an answer to prayer. I'd heard people say God spoke to them, but this was sooner than I expected. I told myself that if the man asked me again, I would seriously consider it. But he was probably kidding, I thought.

In December, he proved the reality of his offer by flying east to meet me. We talked about the job and about what I could do for him by selling his products. All the while, I saw that the job would get me away from my problems. I told him I would consider it, but that I would have to fly out to look over his business before I made a concrete decision. I knew that I would have to go without Jim so I could make up my own mind.

I Started to Pray

I was absorbed in my thoughts about this possibility. By worrying about what I would do, I lost sight of Jim's needs. One evening I looked at him as we ate dinner, and saw that he had lost weight. I saw more lines, creases, and wrinkles on his face than I had ever noticed before. *I put those there*, I thought, and I felt guilty when I looked at him. I had to get rid of the guilt. I would pray about it, as Ruth had suggested.

When I asked God for forgiveness, I didn't feel relief, the lifting I had heard others talk about. I hadn't committed myself to God, I guess; I had only used him for a sounding board. I had taught Sunday school, been in choir, done my part for dinners and rummage sales, but had not jumped in to God with both feet. I had always waited on that, for Jim to go with me—but he never did. Thus I never really committed my life to the Lord. He would forgive me, I thought, if I asked and meant it. But I didn't feel his forgiveness being issued me.

I had to get back to the routine of regular living, so I dove into the Christmas spirit. But the preparations I so loved each year—baking, cooking, decorating—gave me no such joy that year. I let our youngest daughter, Sarah, decorate the tree, even the silver icicles, a job no one could do to my satisfaction. Sarah didn't notice that, in a separate box, my special ornaments had been set aside and wrapped carefully.

I watched her, thinking, *Where will I be next*

Christmas? Here? Will we be together? What if we do split up? Our marriage didn't feel like it would work, and subconsciously, I had put up my walls. *Was it too late for us?*

Mentally, I prepared for the inevitable break. My thoughts and emotions fluctuated, going up and down as if on a seesaw. *It'll be OK. I can make it work.* (Maybe not.) *I'm sick of trying. I'll leave and start again. I can make that work.* (I hope.) *I'll never see the grandchildren again. I can fly and visit them. They'll hate me.* (I can't handle that.) *Mom and Dad will understand.* (They care about me.) *My sisters and brother will blame me; they all love Jim.* (They love me, too.) *Our friends will hate me.* (They'll know he needs them.) *The kids will feel sorry for Jim and go to see him more.* (They'll still love me.) *I'll be OK, even if I'm all alone. God will forgive me.* (I can't go on.) It was as if I took all the pieces of my mind and threw them into the air, catching them as they fell, in a small paper cup.

I flew out to look at the job on a cold, icy, four-degree day in February. As we were landing, the pilot announced that the temperature was a soothing sixty-eight degrees. "I'm sorry it's so cold," my prospective employer apologized as we walked to his car. *This has got to be God's will for me,* I thought. *He knows how I hate to be cold.* I looked over the job, met the other salesmen, and was wined and dined by my maybe-boss and his wife.

After the trip, things got worse at home. Jim

I Started to Pray

knew I was thinking about the job. Actually, I had decided to take it—and I would go alone. It was my chance to start over. I had to figure out how to tell Jim I was leaving, though, and I wished I could slip away silently some Saturday while he worked in the barn.

We went along ignoring the inevitable for a month. All the time, however, I was planning, logically and methodically. It wasn't the best way, and I didn't want to hurt Jim. But in my frame of mind, I was doing what I had to do. Most of the time, since he ignored the problem as well, I thought he didn't care anyway.

One frosty Sunday I went to church, full of confusion and guilt. The sanctuary furnace wasn't working, so we jammed our sparse group of fourteen into a Sunday school meeting room. The substitute pastor stood only two feet from the front row of icy metal folding chairs where I sat. Had I known there would be a guest minister, I would have stayed home.

"Sin," he began, "can be in your own mind. It isn't the sin, but the forgiveness of it that I will talk about today." He was a lively, spirited preacher. My mind nevertheless drifted at times as he paced back and forth, emphasizing points and vitalizing the small congregation.

I've sinned, I thought. *I need forgiveness. Leaving my husband is wrong, I know that.*

"Forgiveness is yours if you ask and are truly sorry," he continued. "Ask one time and it is yours. If you asked your father for a car next Sunday and he said yes, would you ask him again that afternoon, that evening, and every day until the week was up? No! Only one time! When he said yes, you'd leave the subject alone until it was time to use the car."

He leaned forward, locking his eyes into mine, and reiterated. "God is your Father. If you ask for forgiveness, you've got it. Accept it. God forgives you. You need to learn to forgive yourself."

I had chills. He was talking right to me. "God forgives me," I repeated, in a whisper. "And I have to forgive myself." I had been harder on myself, I realized, than God had. I prayed silently, shutting my eyes. "Please, God—help me to forgive myself the way you've forgiven me."

It was only then I felt the release, the lifting I'd been hoping for. God forgives me!

That was another beginning for me. I planned on leaving, but now I needed Jim's forgiveness. I wanted to start off fresh. I had forgiven myself, and I hoped Jim would forgive me, too. I had been hanging my head, trying to "make it up" to Jim and to God, the bad girl trying to vindicate myself by my good behavior. Jim had gone along with that. He let me thrive on my self-condemnation. I had never asked him to forgive me, but after the experience in church, I asked him to so I could get on with my life alone. Everything still wasn't perfect, but at least my guilt disappeared.

I was determined to follow up my November

I Started to Pray

answer to prayer; I wanted that job. One Friday night in March, before we got ready to go bowling, I finally told Jim: I would move out in the morning. I dreaded the blowup that would follow, afraid there would be a big argument, but he didn't say anything. In fact, we didn't talk at all. He figured it was coming, he said. He walked past me, and got dressed to go bowling.

That night was the longest I can remember. We both hurt—agonized—but didn't know what to say. The middle of a bowling alley is not conducive to talking, but neither of us could think of anything to say.

It looked for a moment like Jim was crying. Not him, though, I thought; he'd never been emotional. He threw the ball, rolling it into the gutter and missing the pins—then sat down—all without saying a word. The kidding the guys usually gave him was missing. They could tell from the look and the lines on his face that something was wrong, but they had no idea what. Jim and I went to bed without speaking that night.

I woke up early Saturday morning. I packed two boxes and a suitcase with necessities, and put them by the dining room table. I made the coffee as I always did, and thought of completing the ceremony by waking Jim.

He got up without being called, a rare occurrence.

"Your coffee's all made," I told him.

"I don't want any." *Don't want any? But you*

always start the day off with coffee.

"I don't want anything," he told me, the lines in his cheeks growing into furrows. He looked so old and sad.

He slipped into the blue jeans he'd worn the night before and quietly walked to the dining room, where he sat in the chair at the table's end. Minutes of silence passed, as he tapped his fingers nervously on the edge of the table. It was hard to know what to say. Finally, he spoke.

"I'll go up on the hill so I won't have to see you go. I know that'll be easier on both of us." He paced back and forth. "No, I'll go to the barn, so if you need anything, I'll be nearby to help. . . . I'll go check the gas and oil first. . . . I ought to let the air out of the tires. Do you have enough money?" He walked to the kitchen, then back to the dining room. All the time he paced, I stood still. I had picked up my suitcase and my purse, but I didn't move. I couldn't seem to move.

"Get out of here if you're going," he said. "Do you want me to leave first, so you can? I know you won't do it if I'm here. You're too softhearted."

But my feet wouldn't move. "You understand, don't you, why I have to? There's nothing of me left anymore. I've given it all away to you and the kids. I need to find me."

This was the most important thing we'd ever faced, yet we weren't able to discuss it. Jim was even willing to walk away so I could leave. He

I Started to Pray

never had understood my sensitivity, and in his own way, he couldn't face confrontation either. I knew all these things as I stood there, holding my purse and the suitcase, and staring at the two boxes I had hastily thrown together.

"Do you want me to help you carry these to the car?" he asked. Then, in a sudden mood change, "I won't help you leave—I'll tie you to the table," he laughed, tears in his eyes.

This was not going to be easy. No matter how I thought of doing it, I knew it wouldn't be easy. *That's why I sneaked out last time*, I thought. I stood there a full forty-five minutes, hanging onto the suitcase, my purse dangling from my arm, and I didn't move. My feet would not let me go. All the while, Jim offered solutions: he'd look the other way, he said, go to the barn, go up on the hill to make it easier.

Why couldn't I go? I had a place to live, a job I had accepted, enough of a salary to take care of me . . . still, I could not move. *But God*, I thought, *you told me it was OK. Why can't I leave?*

Then I knew . . . it was not OK with God. He never had said I could leave. He had given me the opportunity to make a new start—but doing it alone had been my idea. Standing there, with my arms and fingers numb, I knew that God didn't want me to go. He had answered my prayer, but I had misinterpreted the answer.

Slowly, I put down the suitcase. Quietly, I said to my husband, "I think we need to talk."

TWELVE
The Encounter

"Talk?" Jim snarled. "What's the use?" He was tired of my indecision, weary of my always controlling the situation. "Why talk about it? You've made up your mind."

My packed suitcase was by the dining room table, but I knew it was time to talk. I'd stood there with my shoes glued to the floor, wanting him to make the difficult task easier. I had prayed that morning that God would help me do what I needed to do, but he was not helping me. I could not leave.

How could I hurt someone face-to-face, someone I wasn't mad at, didn't hate, someone with whom I've lived for so many years? But then, why couldn't I just do it, tell him it's over, forget it? My legs were as numb as my arms.

When he wasn't swearing, yelling, or throwing out sarcastic remarks, I liked him. We had problems, I knew, but would wiping out twenty-three years of marriage fix them? What about the resentment inside me? Would that disappear by my walking away? For the first time, I realized I didn't want to find out.

We had invested so much time, caring, and fun. *Do I really want to toss it aside like this?* I asked myself. *Might I want it back again?* I didn't want to make an unalterable, unchangeable step.

I'd been with the same person all these years. How could I think as if I were alone again? How would I know where I'd left my glasses, where we'd gone to dinner on our last anniversary, camped out in '62? Who else would know about the time we'd gone hunting together, Jim crossing the fence behind me as I caught and left behind the entire backside of my slacks? How could I forget the good times?

All these thoughts bounced in my brain as I repeated, "It's time to talk." A peaceful feeling settled into my heart, calming the confusion within. "We need to talk—really—and see what we can fix here."

Jim looked at me, not believing what he was hearing and seeing. I could imagine what must have been running through his mind. *Talk? She's ready to leave and she wants to talk? What about? Property settlement? The house? The car? What?*

I locked the doors. It was 9:00 A.M. that Saturday when we began. No coffee. We were about to take the first step toward recognizing each other's

The Encounter

thoughts and giving them importance.

"Let's sit on the couch together," I suggested. Here Jim was, ready to face a lifetime of being alone, not knowing what was going through my mind. He had been trying to make the process easier for me, but now he was being led to the couch and conversation at a point when he'd thought it was all over.

Clearly, I knew we had to express ourselves to each other. We needed to see if this marriage could be repaired. I knew God didn't want me to walk out—I was sure of that now. He wanted to see if we could try again. I was still upset over the marriage, the remarks we'd made, the ignoring, the arguing, but I felt secure in God's love. He had reached down while I stood at the table, and nailed my feet to the floor. I'd had plenty of time and opportunity to leave that morning, but I didn't. I *wanted* to, but I didn't. Jim was ready to have me leave, even though he didn't understand why, but I didn't. It was then I knew, God *had* answered my prayer. But could we survive the answer?

We sat on the couch and began. Anything, just to start the conversation. We talked, questioned, probed feelings and moods—touchy subjects, such as my enjoying work more than being at home. We argued and yelled, and I cried. Still, we sat there. The phone rang—eight times—but we didn't answer it. We remained there on the couch, talking, sharing, sometimes accusing, and still we continued. We were getting inside each other.

We questioned one another: Why had we come to this point? What happened to make us want to get away? No, not us—it was me. I was the one. He never would have left—never would have thought of it. He was content with home, hearth, TV. Never would he have upset that applecart. He liked things the way they used to be.

Lunchtime came and went. We continued to confer. I became hoarse—Jim's throat got dry and we whispered. The phone rang again, over twenty times.

At suppertime, he got up and heated some soup. He had hardly been near a stove since we'd been married, except to lift off the coffeepot. We ate and communed some more, still on the couch. I didn't want to get off the couch to eat. I was afraid we would stop talking, and I didn't want to spoil the mood.

For so many years I had wanted this closeness. I never started this kind of conversation, though, because it might have led to an argument, and I hated to argue. I hated to confront, get angry, hear the snide remarks. Inside, I would boil with hateful, nasty retorts, but never speak them. I would be torn up by that time, my stomach churning and swirling. Confrontation did that to me.

But now—I got mad! I even yelled back sometimes, and still we went on. He didn't understand

The Encounter

and I hollered at him, trying to make him see what my mind saw. He didn't. But we didn't stop. My feelings—my thoughts—he was listening to them! For the first time I put into words, out loud, what was inside, buried and resented. Sometimes I'd thought him possessive, rude, selfish, and rough. Still we shared. It kept coming. When one of my remarks drew blood, it got quiet, but not for long.

During our encounter, we talked sitting up—far apart. We talked lying down, far apart. We talked close together and finally just lay there, as I curled into the curve of his body, and we whispered softly to each other.

We got down to the bareness of ourselves. Lying there, fully clothed, our emotions got stripped and naked. My feelings ran the length of caring, crying, laughing, screaming. His didn't change all that much. Once he did get mad, but not like before. I could tell he cared about me. When he complained about some of the things I had done, he was loud but not hateful. Nothing stopped us from talking.

The phone rang again, and still we didn't answer it. The same things were said many times, but it didn't matter. We talked some more. Problems didn't disappear, but were brought into the open where we could see them. We had exposed them, and now we could try to handle them. This was God's will, I knew then. I could feel him there with us, finally, after twenty-three years.

SOMETHING WORTH SAVING

Our "marriage encounter" lasted until 8:00 P.M.—eleven hours of solid talking! Never had I wanted to make Jim angry by talking about my feelings, but on that Saturday I did. He had never seemed to care how I felt, but on that day he did. We shared—we listened. I heard him say things I never realized he felt. He cried.

"Well, what do you want to do now?" he asked, not quite sure of my new mood. "What shall we do about all of this?"

I thought for a moment... then it came to me. We had talked enough. "Let's go to bed," I told him. "Yes," I repeated, "let's go to bed."

"Bed?" he asked. "You want to go to bed at 8:30?"

"Yes," I said, and I took his hand and led him through the dining room. "I wonder who left those boxes and that suitcase out?" I said.

THIRTEEN
Crash Course in Communication

"We need a crash course," I told Nikki over the telephone. She was a counselor to whom Martha had referred me. It was the Monday after our Saturday encounter, and Jim and I had decided to move out of state. I didn't think it would hurt to get in a little counseling, and maybe discover what it was that put us where we were.

"A crash course in marriage communication?" She laughed. "I have books you can take home and read together, but it'll take some time. Come in for an appointment on Thursday and we'll get started."

I made the first visit alone. I wanted to give Nikki the background, to lay out the confusion and frustration. Jim had always said he didn't have any problems, that they were all mine, so I thought I should be the one to explain whatever it was that was "my" problem.

"I don't need a visit alone with any counselor," Jim assured me, so we scheduled appointments together after my first session with Nikki.

"So many times things inside you are buried so deep you may not even know they're there," Nikki said. She quietly listened to each of us.

Family counseling sounded calm and peaceful. Jim told Nikki he didn't need anything counseling had to offer. It was my problem, he said, but he would go if I wanted. The three of us talked.

Jim looked me squarely in the eye. "I don't think you ever believed I loved you—right from the beginning," he said. "Just because I didn't say the words very often, you couldn't seem to believe I felt them. You still don't believe it, and I still love you. I don't know why it's so hard for you to understand. I loved you then; I love you now. To me, it's more important how we act out the love than what we say about it. I'm not a talker. You should know that by now."

Turning to Nikki, Jim continued, throwing his hands in the air, "She never paid attention to what I did. She just listened for words I didn't say!"

This was more depth from Jim than I'd heard in many years.

We went the route of the counselor's books, which were aimed at stimulating conversation about varied subjects. We got stirred up, all right. We argued about the books—not the subject matter—but the books! Like why we were stupid enough to be using them. We sat on the couch side by side and talked about why people sometimes need others to tell them how to communicate.

"We don't need her," Jim said of Nikki.

"We didn't do too well without her," I replied.

And on and on.

You know what? The arguing was fun. For some reason I couldn't understand, I no longer minded the debates, the arguing, the "fights." I was at peace, inside, for the first time in many years. The arguing was a release. There was no bitterness and no attacking, just an exchange of opposing opinions.

So this is what real couples are like, I thought. I had envied other people of the fun they must have had in marriage. I had been convinced they had solutions we never knew about.

I had answers to questions I had not asked. I had God, who was with me daily, helping me remember that arguments are OK and discussions are healthy. He helped me to know that just because I felt a certain way, Jim could not necessarily see that feeling. And if I didn't convey with constant communication the thoughts and feelings that were important to me, Jim would never know what they were. Suddenly, I was ready to do that, and I felt my soul at rest. I had peace within, a quiet in my heart that I'd never had. I wanted to converse, convey, commune.

I also began to see how much I had hurt Jim. I

SOMETHING WORTH SAVING

had God, but all Jim had was me. And there had been a time when he wasn't sure he even had me. He needed to know he could count on me now. He needed to be sure of me.

Things were beginning to sink in. I learned that I liked the old, blunt, say-what-you-mean fellow I married. I enjoyed the honesty of a husband who told me he thought I looked better in a sweatshirt and blue jeans than in makeup and high heels. He thought I was super, and he showed it—not just by saying it. He was supportive, and helped me with my disillusionments about life. Jim was quite a guy! It was time to let him in on it.

"It doesn't make me happier to have you jumping through hoops, doing all the things you think I need, that I thought I needed, to make me happy," I said. "Your *making* me happy doesn't make me happy. We will both be happy because we are, not because we're forced to be."

He accused me of thinking too much. "What do you want?" he asked, resigning himself to another discussion about my confusion.

"I want you to be yourself. That was the person I loved in the first place. I love the fact that you can know, from one conversation, if a person is genuine or phony. I love the fact that you don't go along with surface-only people. I love the fact that you don't need to stop for a beer with the guys. You say, 'No thanks, I want to get home,' instead of having one because you're afraid of

Crash Course in Communication

what they'll say if you don't. I guess I love your strength. The last thing I want to do is take it away from you." After I said all that, he looked relieved. A bit confused, but relieved.

When I had thought he was critical of me, he had only been trying to protect me, attempting to keep me from being hurt by others. When he had acted angry with me for joining too many activities, it was to run interference for me, to make sure others didn't exploit my eagerness. He did not trust most people. I trusted all people. While his way was not mine, I had to remember that mine was also contrary to his.

Communication—what a blessing!

I got to know him better than I had since we were married. Where did I ever get the idea this man did not care about me? I started to see things through his eyes, and what a difference it made. Instead of resenting him, I came to love him more because of the way he was. When he told me to lock the doors and drive carefully back from class, I realized it was because he didn't like my being out alone at night. Instead of getting angry because he insinuated I could not take care of myself, I tuned in to his protective nature. He was trying to take care of the wife he loved.

When Nikki asked how we did with our crash course, I told her it had worked. When she saw us holding hands and smiling at each other, she warned us of the temporary bliss we were enjoying. "You'll come off cloud nine," she said. "What are you going to do then? There will be a time when he won't look like Sir Lancelot anymore and you might expect more than he can give."

To Jim, she said, "She will say something that'll make you mad. What do you think will happen at that point?" She described moods that might occur, and tried to get us to look at life as it would come down the road. "When people hide things for so long, it's hard to break the habit. You're going to have to work at this continuing communication every day."

We knew she was right. I remember hoping she was right. *All this,* I agreed, *will happen. But we can handle it. We can live with reality easier than I've been able to survive all the pretending I've done in the last twenty years.*

Yelling is not the best way, but if it takes yelling that's OK. The world won't stop turning. Small points may be bothersome, but they're only small points—not the real problems. "I think we have to get the next set of books before we can learn how to tone the yelling down to a reasonable roar or a sensible conversation," I told Jim. For us, it was necessary to have the loudness first. I had been afraid of getting my true feelings out, and this "shock treatment" worked for me.

There are as many means of communication that work in marriage as there are marriages. Some couples like to go for walks, take rides, start out the evening with a quiet dinner, or go to a movie. They find out what leads to sharing what's inside them both, and then begin.

One couple I know shares the responsibility. The husband finds out what his wife needs or makes her happy; if it's conversation, he initiates it. His wife doesn't sit back and wait for him, though. She knows it's important to their marriage that they both work at being sensitive to each other daily. They know better than to think tomorrow is another day. They know it's another day lost if they don't work at their marriage.

That wasn't something Jim and I could handle by ourselves—I know that now. I made the mistake of trying to do it all, trying to fix our marriage by myself. I couldn't do it, so I took it to Someone who could. God listened to me, knowing how mixed up I was, and waited until I was willing to listen. Then he talked to me, softly, in a way I could understand. When I had stood in my dining room, holding my packed suitcase ready for the final scene of my marriage, he kept me from leaving.

When I became fully committed to the Lord, I saw what I'd been doing. I had not relied on him, nor turned everything over to him. Things I thought I'd been doing to help God were not for him at all. By taking control of situations, I thought I got stronger. In the end, however, I became weaker. I had depended on Jim, the kids, my mother, mother-in-law, a new employer, and others to show me how much I was worth. When I finally asked God to lead me, I learned how valuable he thought I was.

God healed my marriage. Jim and I would have to apply the ointment and the bandages, but God had worked the healing and had given us the prescription. He had shown me at the final moment, the darkest hour, that I cared for my husband. Love had seemed far away, and I thought I knew how to fix the problem—by escaping. Day by day, hour by hour, I kept convincing myself I could do it. But I couldn't. I didn't even want to.

When I figured out that leaving was not some short-term idea, I didn't want it anymore. I couldn't get Jim off my mind. Even though we'd argued, said things that would never be taken back, I still cared about him. He cared—he was willing to take the first step. He came after me. All the time we'd gone through daily hell, I performed duties I thought were needed and required. I got through.

Looking back, only now can I see the seriousness of our problem. We could so easily have lost it all.

But lack of communication is not the end of a marriage; it's only the beginning. It marks a time to regroup and reassess the relationship and the love. Now, when I recall the problems, the pain, the feelings, the day-to-day torment, the near loss of our marriage . . . now is when I cry.

EPILOGUE
The Way It Is

The underlying truth is this: "What you think you want is not necessarily what you really want."

Leaving home looked like fun, a great idea when I thought of all the time I would have to myself, and how independent I would feel by making my own decisions. Then there came a day when I sat by myself in my own kitchen, in my own apartment, in front of my own small pantry of canned goods, and wondered, *What happened? Why am I here?* There was the time when we sat together in the van, and I questioned, *What problem is so bad we can't fix it?* Finally there had come that day of confrontation and communication, that day I comprehended, *We've got something worth saving here.*

As you sit alone, stirring your own cup of coffee, thinking about the problems in your marriage, you may decide it is worth saving, worth talking about.

It's hard for some of us to break down the walls around our hearts and let others in. But what harm does it do? Why not take a chance on learning something about ourselves? Many of us never see that person inside until we're alone—faced with being the only one around. When I felt badly about the things happening around me, I learned to look at what was inside me. When I found out what was there, God helped me love myself. Only then was I ready to love someone else.

Love is not just talking about love. Love is sharing, understanding, wanting to help by just being there. Until we understand ourselves as God does and realize what he wants for us, that love can be within but we will never see it.

I blamed my marital problems on being married to a nonbeliever. It was an easy out for a "spiritually single" person. I had failed to see that God loves my husband just as much as he does me. If I don't look at Jim as God does, through the Lord's eyes, I'll never know how much Jim matters to God. Worse yet, Jim will never know. We must remember the love God has for each of us as he looks at each of us.

This is the way it is with Jim and me today:

We have learned to communicate. The caring we have for each other is open and out loud—not only verbal, but also actual. Our walls are down.

The Way It Is

"I wish you'd given me a card at least," I said on my last birthday. "Something that says 'I love you' is all I need." Lying on my pillow that night was a piece of notebook paper with Jim's handwriting on it: "I do love you, you know."

We're not afraid to let each other inside. And we're not afraid to let our feelings out. Because of those attitudes, our problems are not shelved. Feelings cannot be buried, only to fester in resentment and bitterness. Once we get the problems, the culprits, out in the daylight, there's nothing to be afraid of.

Sometimes levity is called for. Often it's not. Jim recently sought consultation on some unwanted but necessary knee surgery. As we drove down a busy expressway on a trip to see the doctor, I tried to lighten the atmosphere.

"This may be just the opportunity you're looking for," I said as we discussed the possibility of his being laid up for six months. "This might be a way for you to go into business for yourself, get out of the job rut, to grow and change."

"Easy for you to say!" he retorted. "You're not the one who'll be off your feet and out of work. You're so darned cheerful about everything. Life isn't always like that, you know. It doesn't always work out for the better. You don't have any idea of what the real world is like!"

Many things whirled in my mind. We were driving along at sixty miles per hour, arguing about surgery the doctor said would be necessary.

SOMETHING WORTH SAVING

What choice does Jim have? Why isn't he better at facing problems? Why does he lash out at me for thinking the best? It was true that I was overly optimistic; my friends once said that if the world came to an end, I'd be pleased that at least it was a nice day for it. My cheeriness seemed only to bring out his anger.

I thought about getting out of the car and out of the situation. Why couldn't he see that I was trying to make him feel better? I uttered a silent prayer, "Lord, help me handle this."

The words that came out of my mouth tamed my torment: "You're right, that is the way I am." I smiled, and Jim laughed.

"That's right!" Jim agreed, still chuckling.

Why didn't I try to see the situation from his viewpoint? The surgery would cut him off from everything he knew. He'd been told the job he loved would be out of the question after surgery. Jim had looked at the picture of his future realistically, and it scared him. The last thing he needed was my telling him how rosy things would be.

It's not agreement, but understanding, that makes marriages last. We're not carbon copies of each other, but complements, supporters. When the nurse called us into the inner office, we had to wait another hour. I didn't mind. We got down to serious talk—calm discussion. I told him, "It must be scary, thinking about changing your job-style completely."

"I don't know what else to do," he said.

That's all we needed for a comprehensive, sensitive, caring, sharing conversation. Understanding and response. We talked about how he'd have to take another look at what he could do. There were many jobs that could utilize his knowledge, some of them not so physical that he couldn't handle them.

"What happened," I said to Jim, analyzing our flare-up, "was that you were upset about the surgery. It made you mad, so you took it out on the first and closest thing—me." My talking about these sorts of things used to make him accuse me of thinking too much.

"You're right," he said. "I don't look forward to this. But you're right, I have to look at what else it may lead to."

Our Saturday morning conversations occur more frequently now. Jim and I can look back and see not only progress, but self-sacrificing, blossoming love. "I wish other women realized how hard it is to leave, that it doesn't always fix everything," I told him. "I wish I could let them know that it's a bigger decision than it appears on soap operas. How sometimes it hurts so badly to be alone."

I knew we'd come a long way together when he replied, "Why don't you write it down? Why don't you tell them?"

And that's what I've done.

Other Living Books Best-sellers

THE ANGEL OF HIS PRESENCE by Grace Livingston Hill. This book captures the romance of John Wentworth Stanley and a beautiful young woman whose influence causes John to reevaluate his well-laid plans for the future. 07-0047 $2.50.

HOW TO BE HAPPY THOUGH MARRIED by Tim LaHaye. One of America's most successful marriage counselors gives practical, proven advice for marital happiness. 07-1499 $3.50.

JOHN, SON OF THUNDER by Ellen Gunderson Traylor. In this saga of adventure, romance, and discovery, travel with John—the disciple whom Jesus loved—down desert paths, through the courts of the Holy City, to the foot of the cross. Journey with him from his luxury as a privileged son of Israel to the bitter hardship of his exile on Patmos. 07-1903 $4.95.

KAREN'S CHOICE by Janice Hermansen. College students Karen and Jon fall in love and are heading toward marriage when Karen discovers she is pregnant. Struggle with Karen and Jon through the choices they make and observe how they cope with the consequences and eventually find the forgiveness of Christ. 07-2027 $3.50.

LIFE IS TREMENDOUS! by Charlie "Tremendous" Jones. Believing that enthusiasm makes the difference, Jones shows how anyone can be happy, involved, relevant, productive, healthy, and secure in the midst of a high-pressure, commercialized society. 07-2184 $2.50.

LOOKING FOR LOVE IN ALL THE WRONG PLACES by Joe White. Using wisdom gained from many talks with young people, White steers teens in the right direction to find love and fulfillment in a personal relationship with God. 07-3825 $3.50.

LORD, I KEEP RUNNING BACK TO YOU by Ruth Harms Calkin. In prayer-poems tinged with wonder, joy, humanness, and questioning, the author speaks for all of us who are groping and learning together what it means to be God's child. 07-3819 $3.50.

SUCCESS: THE GLENN BLAND METHOD by Glenn Bland. The author shows how to set goals and make plans that really work. His ingredients of success include spiritual, financial, educational, and recreational balances. 07-6689 $3.50.

MOUNTAINS OF SPICES by Hannah Hurnard. Here is an allegory comparing the nine spices mentioned in the Song of Solomon to the nine fruits of the Spirit. A story of the glory of surrender by the author of *HINDS' FEET ON HIGH PLACES*. 07-4611 $3.50.

THE NEW MOTHER'S BOOK OF BABY CARE by Marjorie Palmer and Ethel Bowman. From what you will need to clothe the baby to how to know when to call the doctor, this book will give you all the basic knowledge necessary to be the parent your child needs. 07-4695 $2.95.

Other Living Books Best-sellers

ANSWERS by Josh McDowell and Don Stewart. In a question-and-answer format, the authors tackle sixty-five of the most-asked questions about the Bible, God, Jesus Christ, miracles, other religions, and creation.   07-0021 $3.95.

THE BEST CHRISTMAS PAGEANT EVER by Barbara Robinson. A delightfully wild and funny story about what happens to a Christmas program when the "Horrible Herdman" brothers and sisters are miscast in the roles of the biblical Christmas story characters.   07-0137 $2.50.

BUILDING YOUR SELF-IMAGE by Josh McDowell. Here are practical answers to help you overcome your fears, anxieties, and lack of self-confidence. Learn how God's higher image of who you are can take root in your heart and mind.   07-1395 $3.95.

THE CHILD WITHIN by Mari Hanes. The author shares insights she gained from God's Word during her own pregnancy. She identifies areas of stress, offers concrete data about the birth process, and points to God's sure promises that he will "gently lead those that are with young."   07-0219 $2.95.

400 WAYS TO SAY I LOVE YOU by Alice Chapin. Perhaps the flame of love has almost died in your marriage. Maybe you have a good marriage that just needs a little "spark." Here is a book especially for the woman who wants to rekindle the flame of romance in her marriage; who wants creative, practical, useful ideas to show the man in her life that she cares.   07-0919 $2.50.

GIVERS, TAKERS, AND OTHER KINDS OF LOVERS by Josh McDowell and Paul Lewis. This book bypasses vague generalities about love and sex and gets right to the basic questions: Whatever happened to sexual freedom? What's true love like? Do men respond differently than women? If you're looking for straight answers about God's plan for love and sexuality, this book was written for you.   07-1031 $2.95.

HINDS' FEET ON HIGH PLACES by Hannah Hurnard. A classic allegory of a journey toward faith that has sold more than a million copies!   07-1429 $3.95.

LORD, COULD YOU HURRY A LITTLE? by Ruth Harms Calkin. These prayer-poems from the heart of a godly woman trace the inner workings of the heart, following the rhythms of the day and the seasons of the year with expectation and love.   07-3816 $2.95.

WHAT WIVES WISH THEIR HUSBANDS KNEW ABOUT WOMEN by James Dobson. The best-selling author of *DARE TO DISCIPLINE* and *THE STRONG-WILLED CHILD* brings us this vital book that speaks to the unique emotional needs and aspirations of today's woman. An immensely practical, interesting guide.   07-7896 $3.50.

Other Living Books Best-sellers

LORD, YOU LOVE TO SAY YES by Ruth Harms Calkin. In this collection of prayer-poems the author speaks openly and honestly with her Lord about hopes and dreams, longings and frustrations, and her observations of life. 07-3824 $2.95.

MORE THAN A CARPENTER by Josh McDowell. A hard-hitting book for people who are skeptical about Jesus' deity, his resurrection, and his claims on their lives. 07-4552 $2.95.

NOW IS YOUR TIME TO WIN by Dave Dean. In this true-life story, Dean shares how he locked into seven principles that enabled him to bounce back from failure to success. Read about successful men and women—from sports and entertainment celebrities to the ordinary people next door—and discover how you too can bounce back from failure to success! 07-4727 $2.95.

THE POSITIVE POWER OF JESUS CHRIST by Norman Vincent Peale. All his life the author has been leading men and women to Jesus Christ. In this book he tells of his boyhood encounters with Jesus and of his spiritual growth as he attended seminary and began his world-renowned ministry. 07-4914 $3.95.

REASONS by Josh McDowell and Don Stewart. In a convenient question-and-answer format, the authors address many of the commonly asked questions about the Bible and evolution. 07-5287 $3.95.

ROCK by Bob Larson. A well-researched and penetrating look at today's rock music and rock performers, their lyrics, and their lifestyles. 07-5686 $3.50.

SHAPE UP FROM THE INSIDE OUT by John R. Throop. Learn how to conquer the problem of being overweight! In this honest, often humorous book, Throop shares his own personal struggle with this area and how he gained fresh insight about the biblical relationship between physical and spiritual fitness. 07-5899 $2.95.

TAKE ME HOME by Bonnie Jamison. This touching, candid story of the author's relationship with her dying mother will offer hope and assurance to those dealing with an aging parent, relative, or friend. 07-6901 $3.50.

TELL ME AGAIN, LORD, I FORGET by Ruth Harms Calkin. You will easily identify with Calkin in this collection of prayer-poems about the challenges, peaks, and quiet moments of each day. 07-6990 $3.50.

THROUGH GATES OF SPLENDOR by Elisabeth Elliot. This unforgettable story of five men who braved the Auca Indians has become one of the most famous missionary books of all times. 07-7151 $3.95.

WAY BACK IN THE HILLS by James C. Hefley. The story of Hefley's colorful childhood in the Ozarks makes reflective reading for those who like a nostalgic journey into the past. 07-7821 $3.95.

The books listed are available at your bookstore. If unavailable, send check with order to cover retail price plus $1.00 per book for postage and handling to:

Christian Book Service
Box 80
Wheaton, Illinois 60189

Prices and availability subject to change without notice. Allow 4–6 weeks for delivery.